Understanding

Understanding

Understanding

Understanding

Humphry Osmond, M.R.C.P., F.R.C.Psych.

with John A. Osmundsen

and Jerome Agel

1817

Harper & Row, Publishers

New York
Evanston
San Francisco
London

FIRST EDITION

Designed by Dorothy Schmiderer

Library of Congress Cataloging in Publication Data

Osmond, Humphry.
    Understanding understanding.
    Includes bibliographical references.
    1. Personality. 2. Perception. 3. Hallucinations and illusions. 4. Schizophrenia. I. Osmundsen, John A. II. Agel, Jerome. III. Title.
BF698.073   153.7   72-11876
ISBN 0-06-013239-6

Contents

Understanding

Understanding

1
Entering Others' Worlds

Differing Perceptions of the Outer World

Pavlov: "This is the eternal sorrow of the world, that no one ever enters the subjective of another."

Proust: "The only true voyage of discovery would not be to visit strange lands, but to possess other eyes, to behold the universe through the eyes of another, of a hundred others—to behold a hundred universes that each of them beholds, that each of them is."

Yevtushenko (in "The American Nightingale"): "All nightingales understand each other, but we men, can we never understand each other?"

Dr. Paul Fejos (late director of the Wenner-Gren Foundation for Anthropological Research): "Everyone thinks he is unique and special, so you must *treat* him as if he's special—and you are right in doing so, because he *is*."

Explicit or implicit in all these quotations is recognition of the fact that the world as it appears to one person differs from the world as it appears to another. We are all occupying the same world "out there," but our subjective assessment of it "in here" depends upon how we *perceive* the "outside world"; and it is our perception of it that motivates our thoughts, feelings, and actions, hence our personalities or personal styles. Individuals perceive the same things differently and, so, *function* differently within the same setting. Have you ever wondered what someone sees in so-and-so, or why you're so fond of someone, or he of you? Have you ever wondered why some people seem unable to get along with each other? Confronted by the same circumstances in the "outside world," people respond differently—and characteristically—on the basis of their different subjectives, or "inner worlds."

One very effective way to see that different worlds exist in different people is to consider how madness, drugs, and lapses in rationality—perhaps leading to violence—can *change* people's "normal" self-worlds. These "changed worlds" will be explored in this book.

With the seemingly infinite variety of individuals in the world, trying to find a way for systematically understanding the self-worlds of all of them—or of *any* of them, for that matter—might seem hopeless. However, as will be shown later, certain constellations of personality traits tend to segregate into a manageably limited number of general characteristics that account for a wide range of functional styles.

There is a corollary to the concept that understanding people requires finding ways of penetrating their personal self-worlds: not only do people with different self-worlds function differently (and people with similar self-worlds function similarly), but different persons require different treatment by others, in accordance with their particular, different self-worlds.

That being true, one is tempted to rephrase Jesus' commandment: "Thou shalt love thy neighbor as thyself." In many cases, loving your neighbor *as yourself* probably will not do well by him or her, if the self-worlds involved are very different. Less ambiguously, the commandment might be rephrased: "Thou shalt love thy neighbor as *himself* or *herself*."

In this way, one would avoid imposing one's own world on another and would support the other's personal style or self-world. People would thus facilitate each other's fulfillment. Your neighbor would have no doubt from your treatment of him in this way that you "understood" him. Moreover, if your neighbor treated you in the same fashion—showing that he "understood" you—both of you would benefit from an increment of *self*-fulfillment through mutual understanding.

Ways of Entering Others' Inner Worlds

This seems reasonable, you may say, but how does one go about understanding another by "penetrating his self-world"?

Though we may not think of it this way, everyone experiences in his lifetime many worlds that are different from his own. One way in which we are able to enter other worlds is through great works of art—literary art, in particular. Art enables us, almost, to experience a particular outlook, mood, or vision from another person's viewpoint (real or fancied). Therein lies much of the thrill of fine literature. It may seem gratifying to read stories about heroes and heroines who think, feel, and dream precisely as one does oneself; however, this sort of romantic resonance is liable to dampen in time. One will seek, instead, characters totally *unlike* oneself, who do, say, and think things one might never imagine.

In that way, art expands our capacities for the sort of imaginative and vicarious experiencing that is necessary to achieve any sort of understanding of ourselves and of others. To paraphrase J. B. S. Haldane's lovely line: Others' worlds may be not only queerer than we imagine but perhaps queerer than we *can* imagine—without some guidance, at least, of which art provides a measure. (Haldane made another observation on "differentness," which deserves attention here: "Natural selection favors a variable response to the environment; were this not so, the world would be much duller than is actually the case.")

But what is it like actually to enter "another world"—without the benefit of art? We all do this some time or other in our lives, though we are not always aware of it. We enter "other worlds" sometimes when we are ill, particularly if a high fever produces delirium. Our normal worlds can also be altered by the use of alcohol, drugs, or other agencies that modify our perceptions. Sometimes great emotional stress can bring about a transformation of outlook, producing a world view that is alien and strange to one's normal self.

Many other conditions will create "new worlds" of altered perceptions that require modifications in a person's behavior. Stroke is an example. The retraining of a person who has experienced such a cerebral accident should begin on the basis of the particular perceptual world that existed for him *before* the stroke. Also, people in their declining years tend to experience increasingly serious disturbances in their perceptual worlds, which make it difficult for them to function as effectively as they could if they were unencumbered by such distortions. Perceptual training might be designed for aging persons who are subject to this sort of difficulty. The aim of the training would be to give the person a little "map" whose coordinate systems would be based upon the individual's familiar perceptual world and would help orient him in a new world of mixed realities.

Recognizing the need for attending to the natural and abnormal differences between perceptual worlds can have immensely gratifying and enjoyable consequences. It is a good feeling to *know* about your own world; this knowledge doesn't give you control of it, but it makes you better able to cope. Unfortunately, much education today doesn't really prepare us for coping; it does not lead us to examine the nature of our particular phenomenal world and its relationship to everyone else's.

One evening in the autumn of 1967, I saw two moons in the sky close together. Intrigued, I mentally trotted through various neurological ailments that might have produced such aberrant vision—multiple sclerosis, cerebral tumor, stroke, some unusual virus affecting the eye muscles. None of these seemed likely.

Then I noticed that the two moons reduced to one when I shut my left eye. As time went on, it got much worse. For one thing, the number of moons increased. When the moon was full, I used to gaze at *them*. Gradually, my right eye registered several moons, too. Soon, I was seeing about ten moons with my left eye and three with my right. Driving became increasingly difficult. I did only as much of it as I had to. I was having trouble reading road signs, and instead of a single white line in the middle of the road, I saw three lines. Although I could always discern which line was which, having to deliberate over it was annoying. The amber, red, and blue directional lights on cars and trucks multiplied so that it began to look like a constant Christmas tree on the parkway. I had difficulty finally in deciding which were the relevant lights to respond to. There was the constant "explosion" in my head of oncoming headlights while driving at night.

I went to an excellent eye doctor who urged me to agree to cataract surgery.

By this time, I was having difficulty seeing people's faces. And I seemed forever to be surrounded by a strange blue haze, particularly in rooms illuminated by fluorescent light. The edges of things were blurring; I could not make out the big letters on a local water tower. Buildings seemed to disintegrate, day by day. Even newspaper print and my own handwriting seemed strange; they did not appear quite as black as they had been, and the paper became grayer and grayer. It was as if all publishers had

there is less and less information, overall, to deal with. By contrast, the person recovering from cataracts must put up with a great *increase* in visual input. The degree of difficulty in adjusting to a "new" postcataract environment depends upon how closely the new images in the incoming visual information correspond to the engrams (or coded representations of the images of observed objects) that are stored in the brain and represent the "familiar" world. Is the engrammed information sufficiently like the new, incoming information to be decoded? The answer is that it is, *and* it isn't.

My family was greatly relieved to have me home. I was so utterly delighted *just to be able to see them all again* that my initial reaction was one of delight alone. However, as time went on, a mysterious uneasiness pervaded the atmosphere for me which *they* couldn't actually sense: it was hard to tell just what was causing it.

Now, had I been an Arab—a person well known for his enjoyment of close personal proximity—this uneasiness might never have occurred; indeed, things might have even seemed pleasantly cozy. But being a cold-hearted northern European *and* a no-contact animal by temperament, the apparent closeness of people was disturbing to me. I didn't *realize* that I was behaving strangely at the time, at least not in any way that was inconsistent with my changed view of the world. The trouble was, of course, that I was functioning in a world that was different from my normal one. What with the magnification and bunching together of people and objects and the foreshortening of space, I felt as if I was living in a small place with very large people in it—circumstances anathema to my nature—and I was simply acting accordingly while my vision was settling down.

My uneasiness continued for several weeks, and its effects spread to others like ripples in a pond. Then, one day, a remarkable thing happened. My optometrist fitted me with a pair of glasses that corresponded in their effects on my vision very well to the bifocals I had had before my eyes went bad. I popped them on at home, and the instant I looked around at my wife, Jane, and the children, I realized that I was seeing—sensing and *feeling*—something quite different from the moment before. They had all *shrunk* to normal size! And so had everything else in my world. My uneasiness also shrank, and soon disappeared altogether.

Not many people who undergo experiences similar to mine have the technical background and interest in perception to help them accommodate to their "new" world effectively. Oddly, this also applies to eye doctors, few of whom have any mind for such matters as the *meanings* of space to an individual and the variation in meanings from one person to another.

There are also certain second-order effects on the individual who sees his family, boss, and other persons changed in various dimensional aspects and in relation to himself. Even his own body will seem to change. His hands and feet may appear to grow 30 percent in size, without *feeling* as if they'd grown bigger. The doctor realizes that the procedures he has undertaken will alter his patient's perception, say, by magnifying everything 30 percent. And he communicates this to the patient. (Sometimes it's the other way around; the patient reacts to his new view of the world, and the doctor then explains what the patient already knows.) But usually little or no attention is given to the immediate and collateral effects of these changes in the patient's familiar world; *he has to find out for himself*. He must rearrange his body and his perception of both himself and other persons in his brain. This line of reasoning concerning my own condition after cataract surgery gave me a clue to what was happening to me, and why.

Gross distortions in the perceptual worlds of persons who are unprepared for them will produce a deep anxiety. Infringement of some people's personal space is distressing and even threatening to them; others may experience no distress but, instead, be terribly pleased. Imagine the distressed person being a pretty girl and the pleased person a socially aggressive young man, both of whom are experiencing altered perceptual worlds like mine. Considerable misunderstanding is likely to arise from an encounter between them while they are adjusting to their "new" worlds.

Consider older women who undergo cataract surgery. What usually upsets them most, after recovering from the operation, is seeing themselves in the mirror. Before surgery, they saw a blurred outline which they filled in with pleasant fancies and memories of earlier years. Suddenly, they see the real person, looking much older, showing every wrinkle and registering distress at the same time. As a result, many such women discard their glasses and retreat to a world of memories.

2
A Typology of Man:
A Key to
Others' Worlds

Need for, and Origin of, the Typology

It is important to take into account individual differences in people when engaging in family, social, and professional relationships. We all say we do this, but the fact is that until now there has been no way—no theory or system—for understanding normal human behavior in terms of identifiable, meaningful personality or behavioral traits or characteristics. Such a theory would constitute a psychological "typology," a systematic categorization of different psychological types for normal human behavior.

A typology of that nature would both *classify* different behavioral types and, most important, *explain why* certain typological traits tend to occur in some individuals. By explaining why a person of a particular type combines certain traits in his personality, the typology should help one to understand him. This, in turn, should enable one to achieve what Pavlov sorrowed over no one's ever being able to do—to enter into the subjective of another and, in a sense, to see the world as if through another's eyes.

In collaboration with two clinical psychologists, my friends Dr. Harriet Mann and Mrs. Miriam Siegler, both of Cambridge, Massachusetts, I (H.O.) had the good fortune to develop a new and different kind of psychological theory: indeed, it is exactly such a typology of normal human behavior as has just been described.[1]

In this Typology, there are sixteen major, different *but equally normal* ways of perceiving, or experiencing, the world. These sixteen "experiential worlds" are based upon combinations of six basic personality traits and differ from each other in many important ways. Conflicts and compatibilities can often be understood more clearly in terms of the differences in people's experiential worlds.

JUNG'S TYPOLOGY

The theory derived its impetus from Carl G. Jung, who introduced the idea of psychological types half a century ago. His typology was complicated and vague, however, and the only part of it that has persisted in the public mind is the concept of Introversion and Extraversion. Less well remembered are the Jungian typology's names for the four functional types (Thinking, Feeling, Sensation, Intuition), which our theory also utilizes.

Jung's *Psychological Types* was published in 1923. His typology—as ingenious as it was for classifying and describing personality traits—did not explain why certain typological traits

1. The Typology referred to throughout this book is based on an original paper, "The Many Worlds of Time," by Harriet Mann, Miriam Siegler and myself, in the *Journal of Analytical Psychology*, vol. 13, no. 1 (1968). Since that paper was published, a book has been commissioned of the three authors by Doubleday & Company and is in progress. The Typology has been greatly elaborated and refined since the original paper, but it would have been improper to use here the elaborations and refinements. Nevertheless, even in the rough-and-ready form described here, the Typology works —as you will see.

occurred together in the same person. Most of his character-
izations of the types were downright simplistic, suggesting that
one type was "exploitative" and another was "cold and detached" but without any indication *why* either behaved sometimes in what Jung saw as exploitative or detached ways. Jung's
failure to endow his typology with explanatory powers greatly
reduced its practical value.

There were other weaknesses in his typology. When one
discusses a typology of human behavior and personality, one
tends to do so from his own bias, and this is what he did. Unfortunately for him, Jung's bias put his system in trouble from
the start, and he was never able to extricate it. Part of his bias
was shaped by his natural bent for pursuing the Platonic concept
of the totality of things; in his typology, this took the form of
what is called "individuation." According to Jung's hypothesis,
an individuated person would be able to express the full range of
typological traits according to his pleasure. As far as I know,
the hypothetical, individuated person who lives *with equal*
facility in all possible experiential worlds has never materialized
(though it is clear that all typological functions are to some degree accessible to us all).

One possible source of Jung's compulsion for Platonic totality
was his belief that he himself was highly Introverted, whereas
—by his own definition—his normal behavior would have to be
characterized as extremely Extraverted. I think he felt he was
demonstrating individuation by *being* one way (Introverted)—
which I believe he was not—and *behaving* another (Extraverted),
which he probably was.

Jung's Introversion and Extraversion are distinguished from
each other by the source from which the individual derives his
values. The Introvert lives within himself and derives his values
more from within than from the world external to him. The Extravert constructs his inner world from information he receives
from the world outside. Functionally, the Extravert relates his

inner being to the outside, and the Introvert relates the outside world to his inner being.

It probably seems the epitome of arrogance to insist that the man who invented the game—Jung's original typology—played it badly, misclassifying *himself*, of all people. Yet this conclusion seems quite inescapable. Jung did not apply to himself his rules with regard to the typological types that he had proposed in his typology. He kept changing his mind about himself, thinking originally that he was one type, then deciding he was another.[2]

Dr. Mann, Mrs. Siegler, and I made a true scientific theory of Jung's typology by giving it explanatory and predictive capacities beyond its capability for simple classification of normal human behavioral types. We did this by incorporating into the Typology the concept of the "umwelt" (self-world), or experiential world. The umwelt idea was presented about forty years ago in a delightful little book, *A Stroll Through the Worlds of Animals and Men*, by Freiherr J. von Uexküll, a German marine biologist.[3] Von Uexküll described the umwelts of a wide range of creatures, from ticks to astronomers, in terms of the temporospatial dimensions that each one experienced in a way peculiar to itself. I believe my colleagues and I were the first to adapt the concept of the umwelt into psychiatry.

2. Dr. Renée Nell had planned to write a book on this in the early 1960s. Unfortunately for its many potential readers, though fortunately for those whom Dr. Nell treats so effectively at her Country Place with a combination of psychological, biological, and typological techniques, she gave priority to her patients above her writings. Because Dr. Harriet Mann had been her research assistant and also her secretary, no one could be better placed to bring to us the fruits of Dr. Nell's years of study of Jung's typology. It is this typology, substantially different from Jung's and from that of most of his pupils, which, when wedded to J. von Uexküll's concept of the umwelt, produced our sixteen types of experiential worlds. I cannot imagine our succeeding in doing this without Dr. Nell's prior work; following discussions with her, it is clear to us that Dr. Nell was not aware of von Uexküll's work and its relationship to her own. Indebted as we clearly are to Jung, we are even more indebted to Dr. Nell.
3. This work is available in *Instinctive Behavior*, ed. by Ch. H. Schiller (New York: International Universities Press, 1957).

Sixteen Types of Existential Worlds

FOUR BASIC FUNCTIONS

One way of avoiding the problems arising from Jung's having overpersonalized his typology in the course of constructing it is to approach the task biologically—say, from the point of view of evolving animal life. It was von Uexküll's work that directed our thinking along this line.

For an animal in the wild to survive, it must be able to focus on current happenings and to "have an idea," biologically speaking, of what has gone before. That is a minimal necessity. The animal must also be able to relate biologically to other creatures in an emotive way as well as according to whatever hierarchy of status and authority ("pecking order") exists for its own kind.

The animal would thus have two ways of functioning. One would focus on the phenomenal *here and now* in response to the discontinuous input to the senses. This style of functioning is called, in the Jungian terminology, "Sensation." The other type of functioning reflects the emotive aspects of life and the continuity of recognition and respect for authority, tradition, and habit in behavior. This continuous function is called "Feeling."

Early humans could probably have managed rather well with only the Sensation and Feeling functions. Sensation would enable them to keep alive by catching food and avoiding predators, and to recognize status, thereby permitting the formation of operational, protective communities. Feeling would equip them to perpetuate their kind by enabling them to look after their young in a kindly manner. Feeling would also help form traditions and ultimately create poetries and sagas. A creature able to function thus would be rather richly equipped.

The existence of a present "now" in the context of a past

"then" implies the possibility of a "thence"—a new "now" when the present one is in the past. The construction, in this way, of a *future* is evidently done by many creatures below man on the phylogenetic scale. The lower animals' future is not an intellectual construct, of course; it is built into behavior patterns such as migration. For example, it is a basic urge of the Arctic tern to fly twelve thousand miles in search of a future that is determined by sidereal events set in train eons ago and stretching away into eternity. It seems likely that early man would have done this sort of future-seeking, too, but on the higher, intellectual level of his unique endowment.

How might an early, intellectual construction of a future proceed? One can imagine that a future would be built out of past experience—recollections, emotions, *feelings*—forged with current experience, or *sensations*. The linearization of feelings from the past and sensations of the present into a projection of the future represents a kind of protothinking.

Thinking, then, is the name of a third style of functioning; it is a logical process of aligning data from the past, data from the present, and projected "data" from the future. The Thinking function distinguishes the *order* of different data, establishes *relationships* between them, and—depending upon biases of various sorts—determines which will be most *useful*. More weight can be given to data from the past or to the data of the present or to anticipated data; which data are emphasized is a matter of the individual's Thinking *style*. This general, logical process is the essence of Thinking.

Thinking and Feeling are both continuous functions. That is, the underlying nature of each is characterized by a particular kind of continuity. In Thinking, the continuity is linear, proceeding logically from past through present to future. In Feeling, the continuity is circular, proceeding from past to present, back to past; the present tends to be regarded as a component of the past sometime in the future, and the future is similarly relegated to the status of a memory at some still more distant future moment in time.

The two continuous functions of Thinking and Feeling conflict with each other. Thinking, being concrete and rigorously logical, reduces one's ability to focus on the pleasures of the emotive aspects of life. Thus, Thinkers are not likely to dawdle over a beautiful sunset or to be the last to leave the scene of a festive occasion but, instead, are prone to "push on with it" and proceed to the next stage in their logical plan. On the other hand, the emotive aspects of life—Feelings—tend to distort Thinking. The Feeler's tendencies to prolong the experience of the moment can interrupt irreparably the Thinker's closely reasoned, logical plan. Nevertheless, conflicting as Thinking and Feeling types can be, they both have important functions in a developing biological society; both types would arise naturally, and niches would be found for them. Inasmuch as these two continuous types incorporate the underlying concept of the discontinuous Sensation-type's focus—the present—neither Feeling nor Thinking conflicts with Sensation, as the former two do with each other.

But those three functional types are not quite sufficient to allow so intricate a being as man to prosper as he has. Additionally, he would have had to be able to adapt to events that bear no obvious relation to the past, that are not obviously deducible from current or past data, and that therefore require actions quite different from those likely to be elaborated by Sensation, Feeling, or Thinking functions. The ability to anticipate change, to direct change and to be prepared in advance for adapting to change would appear to be highly advantageous. A developing society might be expected to favor those individuals who possess such abilities and demonstrate their talents by succeeding where others would fail. This talent for *discontinuous* projection into the future is called—again borrowing from the Jungian terminology—"Intuition."

It is not intended by any means to suggest that Intuition is the supreme functional type. Unlike future-oriented acts of the Thinking-type—which are firmly rooted in the past and present —most purely Intuitive projections fail because they lack those roots, and the future for which they are constructed somehow never comes about. One of the greatest and most powerfully intellectual Intuitives was Leonardo da Vinci. Many of his most wonderful inventions were never realized in his lifetime simply because they required technologies that didn't exist.

Generally, Intuitives tend *not* to accomplish the things that they conceive, because they are unlikely ever to experience their very particular vision of the future. And each Intuitive's vision is indeed very particular. His view of the future is an "original," virtually uniquely his own, because there is no system by which to relate his visions to those of other Intuitives and to reality. Intuitives usually do not understand this, however, and consequently do not look upon their visions as unique. Lacking any conceptual framework for devising the strategies necessary to approach their goals, Intuitives find their gifts thrilling but often rather disappointing. They do not know inherently how to use their gifts, nor is there anyone who knows how to train them to do so.

If Intuition is combined with a capable intelligence in a person who is also lucky enough to have had a good education, and is well turned out socially and is inspiring and cheery, he can probably find a gratifying slot in society. But if the Intuitive is less fortunate and happens also to be rather dull, he will be a nuisance.[4]

4. I know firsthand how difficult the Intuitive's lot can be, for Intuition is *my* primary type. Thinking is my second. (The coauthors of this book, Mr. Osmundsen and Mr. Agel, seem to be Intuitive-Feeling and Thinking-Sensation, respectively—not a bad mix for a three-way collaboration of this sort.) I am not a conceptual thinker at all, but I do have a very wide view of the future. I seem to have a useful knowledge of history and the ability to relate it to events here and in the future. To some, this seemingly *continuous* capability suggests that Thinking would be my first function, and

EIGHT FUNCTIONAL TYPES
(TWO LEADING FUNCTIONS IN EACH PERSON)

Investing the individual with *two* leading functions (in my case, Intuition first and Thinking second) is a modification and extension we made of Jung's typology, besides defining his four types more clearly and explanatorily than he had. Whereas Jung was aiming at what he called "individuation," or the development of all four functions in a single individual, my colleagues and I felt it was unlikely for anyone ever to develop them all *equally* because of the sort of conflicts between types mentioned above in the case of Thinking and Feeling. We did not doubt that a person *could* function according to the style of each of the four functional types if he had to. But we felt that an individual's personal style was more likely to be dictated by a predominant functional type modified by another, secondary functional type. The person's capacities for functioning in the modes of the other two types would be considerably less accessible to him.

In addition, we felt that a person's two primary functions could be combinations of only continuous and discontinuous types; a person's functional style could *not* be shaped by two continuous types (Thinking and Feeling) or by two discontinuous types (Sensation and Intuition), simply because the types would in each case conflict with one another. This meant that

---

not the discontinuous Intuition. However, I'm only demonstrating a fairly good memory and an ability to connect things. When I use my knowledge of history or literature, it is to enhance the picture of the future as I see it, which is often quite different from the view that a fundamentally Thinking-type of person would generate. Occasionally, I suppose I employ this practice as something of a "con," because it is possible to disorganize Thinking-types in arguments by the use of such tactics. I have found that if you are not good at formal logic—and I am not—you must find other techniques.

there would be eight kinds of functional types: Thinking-Sensation, Sensation-Thinking, Thinking-Intuition, Intuition-Thinking, Feeling-Sensation, Sensation-Feeling, Feeling-Intuition, Intuition-Feeling.

EXTRAVERTED FUNCTIONAL TYPES,
INTROVERTED FUNCTIONAL TYPES

Each person is *either* Extraverted or Introverted. Adding those two "attitudinal" traits to the picture brings the total number of possible typological combinations to sixteen. (I would be classified as Extraverted-Intuitive-Thinking.)

Whatever a person's first function was, his fourth would be its opposite in respect to continuity. A primary Intuitive would have Sensation as his fourth function; a primary Feeling would have Thinking as his fourth.

Characteristics of the Basic Types

To appreciate the helpfulness of the Typology, we are going to consider in some detail the special characteristics of each of its functional and attitudinal types and their expression in celebrities of literature, history, and the present day.

But first it is necessary to note what the Typology does *not* do. It does not explain differences in personality as symptoms of psychopathology. It does not reduce the fascinating diversity of human nature to a few repetitive explanations. It does not present so many categories that the system is unmanageable. And it does not present a gloomy picture of tortured souls, struggling to remake their personalities, playing pitiful games with their lives.

Among the things that the typology does do is *classify*. Woodrow Wilson, John Kennedy and Lenin were all Thinking-

Intuitive; Stalin was Sensation-Thinking; Trotsky, Intuitive-Thinking; Iago, Sensation-Thinking; Othello, Feeling-Sensation; Hamlet, deeply Introverted Intuitive-Feeling.

We can now explore the characteristics of each type as expressed in behavior and see how the Typology performs its second major function: *explaining* why certain behavioral traits tend to be associated with certain types.

Let us take first the two *attitudinal* types: Extraversion and Introversion. We know already that they differ in the way they relate to the world: the Extravert relates his inner being to the outside world; the Introvert relates events in the outside world to his inner self. This distinction produces behavioral traits that are best observed firsthand (whereas characteristics related to the four *functional* types can often be discerned easily by merely reading or hearing about a person). An Extravert tends to respond quickly to external stimuli, particularly those that appeal to his primary function. Extraverts are not always gregarious, but neither do they particularly enjoy being alone; the lack of social interaction is regarded as a deprivation. Overall, Extraverts are oriented toward action as opposed to reflection or introspection. Introverts are often hesitant in responding to external stimuli; they need time to integrate the incoming information with their inner being before they respond overtly. They rarely suffer from loneliness. They find solitude a refreshing and welcome relief; it revitalizes the Introvert.

Keeping in mind the temperospatial coordinates of each functional type's characteristic umwelt (Feeling-*past*; Thinking-*past, present, future*; Sensation-*present*; Intuition-*future*), consider how those umwelts predispose individuals of different types to behave characteristically of their leading functions.

Feeling-type. A person with this primary function is fond of memories, reminiscences, diaries, folklore, heritage, and traditions. He does not see a new object or event as being novel, unique, or emergent, but often attempts to relate it, instead, to

must be based upon logic, sobriety, and clearheadedness, the Thinking-type is invaluable. No one can equal him for analysis, planning, and seeing a job through to the end. But having to change course from a plan he had prearranged will tend to disorient and confuse him; this is not a matter of rigidity but of principle. The Thinking-type views a change in plan as denying the guiding power of the logic of time's flow, and, naturally, he resists. Armed with a theory of his design, the Thinking-type will go out to do battle with the world, often ignoring or destroying by logic and wit any "facts" that seem to disagree with his theory. He is usually very articulate, probably more so than any of the other types. He can be creative, systematic, and productive under the right circumstances; otherwise, he may be seen as rigid, narrow-minded, dogmatic, a martinet, opinionated, difficult, arrogant.

Thinking-types include Jefferson, Bernard Law Montgomery, Woodrow Wilson, Franklin D. Roosevelt, John F. Kennedy, Freud, Lenin.

Sensation-type. Concerned with the moment as if it were isolated from the past and future, the Sensation-type is superbly equipped to perceive the present situation in all its shadings and ramifications and to act immediately upon his perceptions. No other type is as effective in dealing with concrete reality; in fact, the Sensation-type's enormous facility for facing an object, person, or event and dealing with it *then and there* often dazzles those who do not possess this ability. His every response is a direct answer to the stimulus presented by the object, person, or event. The mode of operating on the situation is dictated by that situation itself, not by any prearranged plan or commitment or by any regard for either the circumstances in the past leading up to the current situation or the long-range consequences of the action he decides to take.

The Sensation-type is often highly skillful with his hands. He wants to influence his environment, and he does it in a material, physical way. He is often skilled at handling tools and at manipulating people. Ideas, feelings, and inspirations are of virtually no importance to him; he places all his faith in what he perceives with his physical senses. He thrives on crises and emergencies and is very good at dealing with them, in any shape or form. He responds to the slightest cue, grasps the nature of the problem at a glance, and acts without hesitation. Seeing much more in a situation than any other type can, the Sensation-type is able to substitute his ability to read the present in depth for his lack of futurity. Good at handling crises, he should not be expected to devise a five-year plan—or even a five-day plan. Understanding the special nature of the Sensation-type's umwelt—a focus on events and things in the immediate present and not on thoughts, ideas, plans, or intellectual pursuits—will help others avoid labeling him as treacherous or diabolical, which he probably is not. On the other hand, the Sensation-type's mastery of the moment sometimes entraps the Thinking and Feeling types into believing that he is infallible, unbeatable, completely competent. Thinking-types cannot believe a person could act with the skill and assurance of the Sensation-type without having thought everything through; the Feeling-type assumes that the Sensation-type is aware of others' feelings and acts accordingly to avoid hurting them. Neither is true. The Sensation-type likes power and, in the short run, is very skillful in power plays, often outmaneuvering those who devote some of their attention and energy to the past, the future, or the continuity of process.

When two Sensation-types engage, fur can fly. Lacking any concept of the future, the Sensation-type interprets delay in meeting his needs as denial, and he usually tries to maneuver around obstacles to his activity. He needs action; the more of it —in any form—the better. Like the Feeling-type, who prefers good or even bad emotion to no emotion, the Sensation-type prefers a positive, or even a negative, sensation to no sensation. Even Introverted Sensation-types are usually involved in some material activity (if on a smaller scale than their Extraverted brothers): cooking, sewing, tinkering, watch repairing, building shelves, gardening, photography.

Sensation-types include Pasteur, James Bond, Paul Revere, Theodore Roosevelt, Henry Ford, Stalin, Lyndon B. Johnson, Charles A. Lindbergh, Nixon, John Lindsay, Iago, and the heroes of the films *Alfie, Blow-Up, Bullitt,* and *The French Connection* (Popeye).

Intuitive-type. Opposed to the other discontinuous function— Sensation, which perceives the world consciously through sensory mechanisms and responds on the basis of the perceived existence or nonexistence of an object or event—Intuition perceives the world through the unconscious and responds with hunches and guesses. For this reason it is no exaggeration to say that Intuition is the hardest of all types to explain and understand; indeed, our typology is, so far as we know, the only theory that deals with Intuition as a normal experiential world view, instead of as neurotic behavior.

The Intuitive lives in an almost totally hypothetical future and copes with life's vagaries through imagination. Inspirations are his métier. His world is literally chaotic—a dynamic, ever-changing, exciting swirl of action, out of which the Intuitive-type tries to ascertain what is possible; he cares less for what "is" or "was" or even "will be" than for what "could be" or "should be." The present is a mist, the past a shadow, but the future is all warmth, sunshine, bright lights, excitement, fulfillment— and all just beyond the next bend in the road, on the other side of the mountain, tomorrow, next month, five years from now. Enjoying the chaos of his promising, unpredictable world, the Intuitive-type resents and resists attempts by others to impose order. Intuitives reject the "mundane" logic of the Thinking-types and mistrust the emotional commitment and constancy of the Feeling-type; the status, power, authority, and respect that appeal to the Sensation-type are almost completely meaningless to the Intuitive, whose realities are anticipation and visions. The Intuitive frequently seems impatient, registering frustration at having to wait for events to catch up with what—to him—is already clear and apprehendable. Reminding him of the mere existence of time is an annoyance because those who would remind him never experience the flow of time quite as he does: backward, from the future into the now.

The Intuitive thinks and acts quickly, urging others along to catch up with him. Sometimes, in apparent efforts to "take up the slack," he skips about rapidly from one activity to another. While others are "plodding" along, trying to catch up with the vision the Intuitive has shown them, he has probably already abandoned it in favor of a new inspiration altogether. He seldom follows through on a project enough to see if his vision was right or wrong. Sometimes when he is right, it is an intelligent Sensation-type or Thinking-type who reaps the fruit of the seed that the Intuitive has sown. Understandably, the Intuitive tends to be impatient with details and is often quite incapable of handling them. Intuitives can be very entertaining (a party without one is the worse for it) in their efforts to create excitement around them so that the external world becomes as exciting, fast-moving, and chaotic as their interior life is. This type is often very persuasive and inspiring; "charismatic" is an appellation more often applied to Intuitives than to any other type. Always plunging into the future, the Intuitive frequently fails to master the necessary skills of any activity. He is likely to read the first quarter of a book, see the implications of the theory being discussed, and then proceed directly to elaborate upon them himself without ever having finished the book. Consider this thumbnail sketch of a typical Extraverted Intuitive, Leon Trotsky:

He possessed the gift of employing, combining, displaying his small-ish acquisitions in the show window so that people would get the idea that behind it was a well-stocked store. But he was capable of feelings of shame afterwards and of fierce self-depreciation when he found that there were others who had really mastered the books he but pretended to know. . . . He tackled Mill's *Logic*. . . . In like fashion, he dipped into Lippert's *Evolution of Culture* and Mignet's *French Revolution*, only to abandon each of them unfinished. For several weeks on end he was a follower of Jeremy Bentham, assuring all who would listen that . . . [Bentham's writing] was the last word in human wisdom and the formula for all of man's problems. Before he could make a single convert, he himself had abandoned Bentham for an equally brief discipleship of Chernishevski.[5]

Well-known Intuitive-types include Alexander the Great, Joan of Arc, Hitler, Che Guevara, Timothy Leary, Lord Nelson, Marshall McLuhan, Marc Chagall, Charles Darwin, Albert Einstein, Abraham Lincoln.

5. B. D. Wolfe, *Three Who Made a Revolution* (New York: Dell, 1964).

3

Applying the Typology

There, then, is the Typology, described as briefly as comprehensibility would allow. Using the Typology is another matter. Once you get the hang of it, you will probably find it enlightening and amusing, and also, at times, rewarding in a very practical sense. Applying this theory to, say, the behavior of your spouse or your boss or even yourself could go a long way toward explaining why you are having difficulty with a certain person, or he with you, or you with you, and perhaps also toward launching you on the best approach to take for resolution of the difficulties.

Forgiveness and Appreciation

One of the first and most valuable lessons you will probably learn in applying knowledge of the Typology to your relationship with others is simply forgiveness. You will probably feel yourself compelled to forgive a person with whom you are having difficulty, both for not being the way you are and for being the way he is. Forgiveness of the sort that will help the relationship cannot come from simply conceding that "people are different," for everyone pretty much "knows" that; forgiveness of a useful, constructive sort can come only from understanding *how* the other person differs from yourself.

For example, a man may be of a visionary nature, given to theorizing and planning in a very detached way, deliberate and careful, perhaps a little slow and "fussy"—as an Introverted Thinking-Intuitive-type might be. His wife may be quick, active, and impatient with the slow pace of events, wanting always to "get everything out of the way" at once, feeling hurt or angry or both whenever her wishes are frustrated or her feelings seemingly ignored—as an Introverted Sensation-Feeling-type might be.

He will find her "superficiality" and "inconsistency" exasperating, and he will probably be hurt by her lack of any show of interest whatever in his plans and theories. She will be just as exasperated over his plodding pace, his insistence on explaining in elaborate, *logical* detail all the "great theories" that he articulates in various forms, seemingly endlessly, and his failure to "understand her feelings" or at least simply to "accept" them once in a while as being *hers*.

Clearly, a couple of their disparate nature *can* look forward to an utterly miserable existence together if they do not understand each other's nature and "appreciate" their differences. "Appreciation," in this sense, means a special kind of forgiveness by which one individual knows both what to expect and what not to expect from the other, accepts it, and thus—by informed, realistic anticipation—avoids or diminishes disappointment. The couple who function together in this way never have to say they're sorry. Appreciation of this sort can also lead to constructive coalitions of different typologies, as will be shown later.

All of these "rules" apply with children, too. Typological

characteristics are *apparent* early in children—after when they are still mere infants. Knowing that members of the same family can be very different typologically, parents can learn early to "forgive" their children for not being more like themselves and can develop rapport with them by understanding the qualitative differences among the subjective worlds involved. Some parents feel guilty—deep down—for not really "liking" a child of theirs. The actual trouble probably is that the child's world is not only very much different from theirs but different in a way that is not highly compatible with theirs. It would hardly be surprising, for example, for a parent with strong Intuition and Feeling functions to find a child with strong Sensation and Thinking functions just a little hard to take. Understanding the different way in which the child sees the world and functions in it can go a long way toward helping father or mother to "forgive" the child for not being like himself or herself and to love the child more freely than might otherwise be possible, and to *respect* the child for the qualities he or she possesses (and which the parent may not).

Children, incidentally, find the Typology fascinating fun and often, quite early, show surprising facility in applying it—depending somewhat on their own type, of course. Because of its "novelty" and its apparent "arbitrary" nature of pigeonholing human beings, Feeling-types—particularly older ones—tend at first to dislike the Typology intensely; in time, however, if they overcome their dislike of it, they often become the most adept of all types at using it.

How to "Type" a Person

But how do you figure out what a person's classification is?

The task is first to determine the individual's primary and secondary functional classification. The attitudinal traits, Introversion and Extraversion, are important qualities, too, but less so than the functional ones in understanding another's personal style. In any case, a person's attitudinal type will probably become apparent after his functional type is determined.

In many instances, an individual's personal style is clearly expressed in his everyday activities, his likes and dislikes, the sort of job he has, his hobbies (if any), and his general outlook on his world. It is often possible by merely listing a person's most salient traits—both positive and negative—to identify one or even two functional types that correspond to his special characteristics. Similarly, it is usually possible to exclude one or two of the functional types because they clearly do not fit the person's style.

Say, for example, that someone is considered "a man of action" (Sensation or Intuition), enjoys each moment or hates it (Sensation or Feeling), is very warm and empathetic (Feeling), is very effective in handling or manipulating people (Sensation or Thinking), builds model replicas of World War I and II airplanes (Sensation and Feeling), shows immense loyalty and patience with other people on occasion (Feeling), and shows a keen appreciation for status and authority (Sensation).

This skimpily created hypothetical person appears to share traits predominantly from two types: Feeling and Sensation. He clearly does not possess any prominent qualities which would give him a strong Thinking function; Intuition also seems weakly represented. Therefore, one could conclude that the person was a Sensation and Feeling combination. But would he be Sensation-Feeling or Feeling-Sensation? That is, what is the person's leading, or primary, function? The answer is determined by whether he shows more characteristics of continuity or of discontinuity. (Both predominant functions in a person cannot be continuous or discontinuous; there must be a combination.)

We deduce that our hypothetical person must feel some link with the past, suggesting the continuity of the Feeling-type, but does this link predominate? We note that he pays great mind to remembering birthdays, anniversaries, and the like—and becomes very upset when other people forget these "important" occasions. This would also suggest continuity. He is usually deeply upset when *he* forgets a date or personal historical observance of some sort and marks it off to distractions in his life, daily pressures, and the enormous burden others impose on him for help and guidance in the daily routine. He is beginning to look a little less continuous, shifting toward Sensation. And, as it turns out, he *does* have "lapses" in memory, most of them trivial, some of them seemingly happening from moment to moment. There are times, in fact, when he is absorbed in one particular task and behaves in a seemingly "scattered" fashion with regard to other events and situations surrounding him. This is strong evidence that his personal style is *discontinuous*. Thus, our hypothetical person is probably Sensation-Feeling. His fourth and weakest function—always the opposite of the first—is Intuition, leaving Thinking as his third function.

With regard to his attitudinal type, remember that he is a man of action, which would suggest Extraversion, although Sensation-types are also described as such. The question is, how action-oriented is he? If a great deal, it would augur for Extraversion; if not, Introversion, which "diagnosis" would also be supported by his model-airplane hobby. Also, *how* good is he from an emotive standpoint at sizing up people and the circumstances in which they are involved? Finally, how good is he in manifesting some sort of personal influence over the actions of a group? We know he has some facility along these lines from his two functional types, but how much? If he has a lot of "moxie" in this way and tends to act quickly, Extraversion is probably his attitudinal style; if he has a lot of seeming potential for this sort of thing and tends to be hesitant in his actions, he is probably Introverted.

Putting the Typology to use should not be made to appear too simple, for it can be tricky with certain individuals. However, by "playing" with the theory underlying the Typology and applying it to people you know or know of—even yourself—you can develop facility in classifying them correctly in the Typology.

Developing One's Weaker Functions

The fact that one's typological nature manifests itself very early and does not change throughout one's development suggests strongly that hereditary factors are somehow involved. This would mean, of course, that whatever your Typology is, you are "stuck with it" for life. However, you are not prevented from improving your performance in the areas of your two weakest functions, either deliberately or inadvertently. Efforts of, say, an Intuitive-Feeling-type to develop his Sensation and Thinking functions can be exceedingly rewarding, as painful as it may be for one to learn to function in unpreferred modes. Consider the following example, a Mr. F.

As a boy, he wanted to become a newspaperman. This is an admirable ambition but, unluckily, one not particularly well suited to an individual of his typology: Extraverted Intuitive-Feeling. Newspaper reporting and writing make heavy demands on one's ability to solve problems quickly, organize facts, plan strategies for obtaining and producing news stories, use words clearly and concisely, and operate a typewriter and telephone dexterously, as well as on several other talents that endow the Sensation and Thinking functions.

Not only is the Intuition-Feeling (NF)[1] combination deficient in those abilities (as compared with the Sensation-Thinking combination, anyway), but certain qualities in which this type does excel are either irrelevant or anathema to sound journalistic practice. The NF is fanciful, tends to flit from project to project

1. "N" for Intuition, as we are using "I" for Introversion.

(infrequently not finishing them), cares deeply about theories and people and tends to become personally involved with them, and abhors schedules and deadlines. One wonders why such a person would want to inflict himself on the journalistic profession. The answer in this case seems to be that Mr. F. saw the newspaper as a base from which to expand his contact with the world, a place at which something was always happening—excitement, fun, promise, fulfillment—and from which he could *make* things happen. He would be reaching great numbers of people with "the word," which would affect their lives (and his, in consequence). Mostly, newspapering was seen by him as an open-ended adventure, loaded with possibilities for him to explore and, sometimes, to develop into bright realities. (It should be added that these attractions for an Intuition-Feeling person hold very little appeal for the better-suited Thinking-Sensation combination, who is attracted to newspapering for other, more immediate and practical reasons.)

Mr. F.'s problem, then, was to find a way of realizing his dream of becoming a newspaperman in spite of poor natural qualifications. The most direct solution, of course, would have been for him simply to develop facility in his weakest (Thinking and Sensation) functions. He did not know about the Typology when he started out (it didn't then exist in its present form); but somehow he "intuited" a need to learn to function in ways that were uncharacteristic of his personal style, and he did.

The end of the story is that Mr. F. became a journalist, working for leading newspapers on both coasts, two national news magazines, and network television. He became surprisingly proficient in operating from the preserve of both the Thinking and the Sensation functions—spotting news stories, conceiving and planning features, solving immediate problems of obtaining information, organizing story material, writing quickly and comprehensibly. He feels he has been repaid many times over for the agony of self-imposed discipline to develop these abilities, both by his rewarding experiences in the journalistic profession and by the many pleasures and advantages in other activities that his development of his Sensation and Thinking functions have enabled him to enjoy. The rewards are no less enjoyable for Mr. F.'s having solved his problem without understanding the Typology; he feels, however, that if he had known what he was actually trying to accomplish—which knowledge of the Typology would have permitted—the task would have been made easier, a little less painful, and probably a lot more fun. He doubts, however, that even a thorough understanding of the Typology would have made him like schedules and deadlines any more than he does now or ever did.

Each Type Best in Some Situations

Before citing further examples of practical utilization of the Typology, I want to make one thing perfectly clear (as a well-known Introverted Sensation-Thinking-type is fond of saying). No type is intrinsically superior—or inferior—to another. Each has certain advantages and certain shortcomings in comparison to the other three types. One type, or pair of types, may be best for a person in a certain line of work or in certain social situations; the opposite type, or pair of types, may work more to his advantage under other circumstances.

I believe I can best illustrate this by analogy. There is a game I know called Chin, Chin, Chin—Chinique. It has many other names and is said to be very old. Three hand symbols are used. Closed fist represents stone, open hand represents paper, and fingers in the V formation represent scissors. Two players hold their hands behind their backs and say, "Chin, Chin, Chin—Chinique"; then each advances simultaneously whatever symbol he chooses: paper, stone, or scissors. The winner is the one whose symbol controls the other's. Stone can blunt scissors,

scissors can cut paper, paper can wrap stone. All three are valuable, but in different ways—each must give ground on occasion.

Many typological situations correspond closely to this game
and nicely illustrate the point that there is no such thing as
intrinsically successful or unsuccessful types, or intrinsically
better or worse types: there are simply *contexts* favorable to one
and unfavorable to another. In the scissors-paper encounter,
scissors always wins; but scissors always loses against stone. Yet
stone always loses to paper. If paper were pasted on sheet steel,
scissors would again be in trouble because it would doubtless
be blunted by armored paper. But armored paper would probably
not be able to wrap stone any longer, and so on. In a three-
player game of Chin-Chin, two can gang up on the other and
coordinate their symbols; they need never lose, and they very
greatly increase their chances of winning!

Value of Types That Complement

The value of the complementarity of personality types is not
always recognized, even by very intelligent people who have
a good grasp of the Typology. All of us at some time aspire to
omniscience, less often to omnipotence. Both aspirations are mistaken. I have a friend, an Extraverted Intuition-Feeling-type,
whose wife is, most luckily, a highly intelligent, immensely
capable Introverted Sensation-Feeling-type. It would seem reasonable to expect that her judgment in matters belonging to Caesar
would be much sounder than his. Unluckily, silly sex roles come
into play. The all-American boy knows the real, hard, tough,
red-blooded world of business, political affairs and so forth, and
into these sanctuaries of male competence even the all-American girl must not venture. This man's particular all-American
girl combines beauty, elegance, and enormous organizational and
empathetic skill. If I want to know whether a person within our

orbit is straight or not, I ask her. If she said that so-and-so "smells like a crook," I would take heed of this even if she didn't in the least smell like a crook to me. She has a much better sense of smell in these ways than I or, I think, her husband. They would make an almost unbeatable coalition—if only *he* realized it.

It is important that people understand the enormous advantage to be gained by *typological coalitions;* these can add much to the fullness of life. My beloved friend Aldous Huxley, in *Point Counter Point,* has the hero, Philip Quarles, the Huxleyian Thinking man, describe his relationship with his wife, Elinor. Elinor was Philip's dragoman, and brought back to him news of worlds of passion and sensation that he had never entered from his world high up in the ivory tower. This situation corresponds very well to Aldous's relationship with his first wife, Maria, who drew his attention to "Feeling" more effectively and consistently than D. H. Lawrence had done with his ideas of the wisdom of the blood.

Examples of Practical Utilization of the Typology

An example of practical utilization of the Typology can be easily constructed in the field of politics. For a political organization to continue very long, it needs officers who have some idea of social continuity. For officers you may want Thinking people who will carry out the *principles* of the organization or Feeling people who exemplify the *traditions* of the organization. Both have their strong and weak points. A collaboration is ideal!

The essence of the Thinking person is his absolute dedication to the view that he has derived the principles necessary to guide the enterprise. Thinking-types, such as Marx and Lenin, devote their lives to great enterprise, and they do it in a way that is notable—in terms of a theory. They are very clear about this. They maintain that the future behavior of their society and of their political party *will accommodate to this theory*. Often, their theories lead them astray.

Lenin is an outstanding example of the primary Thinking-type's overcommitment to his theories. Whenever he put his political theory to the test, it proved to be, at most, less than successful. He wanted to form a political party that was not heavily contaminated by tsarist informers; at one time his party's Central Committee held practically a majority of them. According to Lenin's theory, war was inevitable; one might, therefore, suppose that he was ready for it when it came. Yet when World War I broke out, he was on a walking tour in the Dolomites, was imprisoned, and might have been shot as a Russian spy by the Austrians! Indeed, he was released only because the Socialist mayor of Vienna said that Lenin was a greater danger to the Russians than he was to the Austrians.

Lenin's theory *was* correct, but his Sensation function was not sufficiently strong to draw his own attention to the immediate dangers that were developing. Later on, when the Revolution finally came, an exiled Lenin was daydreaming and gloomily pessimistic in Switzerland. Only a few weeks earlier he had told his friends that he doubted whether he or they would ever live to see the Revolution. After the Revolution, his many difficulties as an administrative leader arose because he had practically no experience in government. He had devoted all his energies to studying the *theory* of government, and none to the *practice* of governing. His theories told him that the practice and process of governing were merely bureaucratic routine matters that anyone could do and upon which one should not waste time. He discovered at great personal cost that this was not so.

Thinking-types tend to be the great theorists and planners. If their second function is Intuition, as in Lenin's case, they tend to produce immense abstract theories to which they are strongly devoted. This made Lenin deeply revered, but probably not deeply beloved. He was known to be a learned man, and Russian peasants greatly esteem learned men. It is difficult, however, for people to feel warmly toward a person whose typological qualities tend to render him ethereal, detached, and cold.

It is a different matter to combine Thinking with the other discontinuous type, Sensation. There are two very good examples of Thinking-Sensation Englishmen: one of them is the marvelous Field Marshal Montgomery, who was called by the great military critic Sir Basil Liddell Hart "the thinking general" —the first in England since the Duke of Wellington. Montgomery has shown a high degree of continuity of the Thinking sort. Having lost most of his friends in 1916, in the barbed-wire fields of World War I, Monty continued to plug along at his profession through the next twenty years, a relatively unknown, quite academic soldier, teaching younger soldiers about war. While almost no one took any notice of him, he steadfastly devoted himself to working out the practical principles of war. It was only by great fortune for him, so to speak, that he was able to put them into practice. Putting them into practice represented his second function, Sensation.

Montgomery is an Introverted man, but his Thinking-type principles sometimes made him behave quite otherwise. When he went to North Africa, he found that the only general the British soldiers ever talked about was the Nazis' Erwin Rommel, the "Desert Fox." He realized at once that this would have to be remedied, and proceeded to hold a series of meetings with his soldiers in which he put forward his plans in the briefest, most straightforward way. No other general had ever done this with them. Monty explained that he was preparing to defeat Rommel and that they would soon have evidence of this. The soldiers were understandably skeptical; but his success in the battle fought on the fringes of the Quattara Depression, before the battle of El Alamein, convinced them that they had a new type of general over them. Montgomery has described how, on the night of that great and decisive battle, having made his plans, he went to bed at his usual time, 9:45 P.M., just before the bombardment began, so that he could get a good night's sleep and be in the best of shape when the soldiers "handed him back the battle two days later." This is a splendid example of the practical detachment of a Thinking man. More romantic generals would have wanted to be in the thick of the battle with their men. Not so with Monty—he was thinking of his duty to his plans so that he could reduce the number of his soldiers killed. Many soldiers came to owe their lives to this capacity for humane detachment.

Later accounts of Montgomery, many of them critical, always emphasize the extraordinary confidence his soldiers had in him. Since he wasn't a particularly popular man, this was all the more noticeable to observers, friendly or otherwise. Montgomery did not necessarily warm his soldiers' hearts, but they had an enormous respect for his great technical skill and his determination not to waste their lives.

Monty's penchant for planning raised difficulties in his relationships with men of different types who did not understand this quality. In Normandy, he developed a plan by which he was to take exactly ninety days to reach the Seine. The plan produced extraordinary anxieties in both the British prime minister, Winston Churchill, and the Supreme Allied commander, General Eisenhower, both of whom were, basically, unplanning men. Montgomery was confident and cheerful because all was going according to plan; but the other chaps, who didn't understand planning at the gut level, were extremely uneasy—until the battle was actually won.

After the war, Montgomery devoted himself to writing a history of wars, comparing all the styles of war, thereby demonstrating his continuous nature. He constantly reiterated what the principles of war are, and with great skill and ability compared the principles of one army and another.

The other good example of the Thinking-type Englishman— very similar, in fact, to Montgomery—is Edward Heath, the prime minister. He is so much a man of principle that at times he actually dismays his own political party. Heath seems to believe that there are certain immutable principles of government, which he has deduced from his observation of political affairs. During the election campaign he declared that he intended to govern according to those principles. Much to everyone's surprise, he proceeded to do exactly that. Even more astounding, his merely being true to form led people to say how absolutely extraordinary this was. Heath didn't think it extraordinary, of course; for it would strike him odd if you say you're going to govern a particular way and then do *not* govern that way.

Viscount Montgomery did much the same when he said that he was going to reach the Seine on the ninetieth day. He was much surprised at the worry Churchill and Eisenhower expressed over the outcome of the campaign at the time of the battle of Caen. It was only the fortieth day—Monty still had fifty to go. Churchill's and Ike's distress was probably a result of their never having lived to a plan themselves. They simply had no idea that there were men in the world who did. Why? Quite likely because neither was a Thinking-type. And only Eisenhower shared Montgomery's Sensation function. Ike was one of the Feeling-Sensation-types—and certainly one of the noblest. On the other hand, Old Winston was one of the great poetic men produced by the Feeling and Intuition combination.

One may wonder what the reverse Typology of Montgomery and Heath—the Sensation and Thinking combination—would be like. A shining example is the highly Introverted Richard M. Nixon. Eisenhower characterized his vice-president on a number of occasions as "too political." Almost no news commentator has ever failed to pay tribute to Nixon's primarily political nature, the manipulativeness of which is a hallmark of the Sensation-Thinking combination.

Political instincts of the keenest sort stem, first, from the individual's inclination to concentrate heavily on current phenomena—the "now"—and, second, from his highly developed ability to order the present in terms of thought rather than feeling. Accordingly, whatever data come in are processed according to what one might call "short-term theories." This results in behavior that is highly responsive but does not reflect deep emotional involvement.

Lyndon B. Johnson, in contrast to Nixon, combined Sensation and Feeling functions, and was known for emotional outbursts. In his manipulations when he was a senator, LBJ not only twisted people's arms but touched their hearts. Mr. Nixon possesses none of that skill. He is an immensely shrewd man, but he combines an absence of Feeling function with extreme discontinuity. What other sort of man could say he's quitting politics forever—"You won't have Nixon to kick around any more"—and then come back as president?

One of the great difficulties with politicians such as President Nixon is that their manipulative capacities tend to produce distrust. People tend to feel that the manipulator, so acutely aware of what is going on and so skillful at manipulation, is not taking into account people's feelings or the long-range consequences of his acts. And they are right! Nevertheless, many of the standard views about Mr. Nixon are extremely unfair. The record does not suggest that Mr. Nixon is a villainous man. Far from it. But neither is he a man who is likely either to warm the cockles of his country's heart or give "the people" great visions.

John F. Kennedy presented still another combination of functional types: Thinking and Intuition. He was a cool man and had wonderful élan. He was also very detached. But his detachment didn't make people feel he was any less charming. He was detached partly, of course, because he was concerned with other things, and he had good reason to think he could charm people out of being annoyed by his coolness. Indeed, he had both the Intuitive charm and the Irish charm—which is something another Thinking Intuitive, Lenin, did not benefit from.

Robert and Edward Kennedy can also be thought of as political types but types different from their older brother. They represent the two Feeling-types. Bobby was probably Feeling-Intuition. When his feelings were hurt, or he was worried and upset, he tended to be extremely "smoky" and passionate, reflecting his Feeling function. His secondary Intuition function came out in his visions and his dogged commitment to them, even though he was not always clear about what he was committed to. This type can also be terribly vengeful. RFK's pursuit of Jimmy Hoffa, the labor leader, may have been absolutely necessary for the benefit of the country. Still, one couldn't help feeling there was an element of vendetta in it. Further, RFK's and LBJ's seeming inability to get along probably resulted from the conflict between Kennedy's Intuition and Johnson's Sensation functions. These two types are extremely unlikely to get on very well, particularly in politics, where a commitment to tradition precludes engagement in open warfare, in which animosities over innate differences in point of view could be released.

Edward Kennedy, "Teddy," is Feeling-Sensation. This type is exceptionally good at enduring misfortune, and he *has* stood more than his share. (Another Feeling-Sensation type was Othello. When the Moor was charming Desdemona—another Feeling-type—he told her of his difficult early years, and concluded that Desdemona "loved me for the dangers I had passed, and I loved her that she did pity them.") The day may come when the country will love Teddy for the dangers he has passed, and he will love the nation that she did pity them. This is almost irresistible stuff, even against the background of his cheating on a Spanish examination at Harvard and the Chappaquid-dick matter.

Edward Kennedy may not always quite come up to snuff, but we do not really expect him to be a Jack. We do see in him a kind of plodding decency, a solidity. If he is around long enough politically, it will be surprising if he is not elected president. And the reasons for his election will be quite different from those he may enunciate in the campaign.

4

The Special Worlds
of Space-Time

Differing Perceptions of Space and Time

As we are reminded so often by the physical scientists, we live in a "space-time continuum," a world of space and time. Astrophysicists express the basic unit of space measurement in the universe in terms of time—a "light-year," the distance light will travel in one year's time. In fact, physical scientists seem not keen to distinguish between space and time at all, except under circumstances where it is absolutely necessary. There is a reason: to distinguish time and space is often extremely difficult because so much of our experience brings time and space into very close relation with each other. They seem sometimes even to overlap and merge.

In some cultures, space is regularly discussed in terms of time. Inhabitants of the English countryside say that a particular place is about ten minutes' walk away. This may mean anywhere from a quarter-mile to two miles. In the Andes, time is often measured by how long it takes to chew a quid of coca leaf; sometimes the destination is so many cigarettes away.

Social anthropologist Edward T. Hall has recorded many examples of culturally biased perceptions and uses of time and space. What is "punctual" to a Mexican is unforgivably late to an eastern seaboard North American. What seems a "friendly" social distance to a congenial South American is quite likely to cause a North American to waltz around the room backward as a result of a cultural misunderstanding about the space envelopes that people occupy socially; by repeatedly invading the North American's "social space," the South American keeps the other constantly on the retreat.

Many people lack the fundamental ability to see in three dimensions. Depth perception depends upon having two eyes that present two slightly different images of an object to the brain. The fusion of the two images gives the sense of depth. Clearly, then, the loss of one eye, or its failure to focus upon the same object as its fellow eye, will result in loss of depth perception. A variety of changes along the optic pathway to the brain or in the brain itself will produce much the same effect. People differ considerably in their capacity for binocular vision. In certain occupations, such as flying, in which depth perception is extremely important, elaborate tests for it have been developed. Having good binocular vision is also an aid in driving an automobile. Those who lack binocular vision perceive space and the objects in it as two-dimensional. They get along in the "real," 3-D world by making certain adjustments in responding to their deficient perceptions.

Many people also see space as having greater or lesser *social* reality. Some of us are extremely good in recording spatial configurations in our brains. Such people can sometimes find their way unerringly—like homing pigeons—across uncharted territories. Others have considerable difficulty in finding even routes that are "well known" to them; this is not a simple matter of "forgetting." Space, for them, has a different *social* meaning from the one it has for other people who learn a territory with extraordinary speed and skill. Typologically, persons strong in territorial functions—Thinking and Sensation—are likely to be the "homing pigeons"; persons weak in those functions and strong in the unbounded ones of Intuition and Feeling are repeatedly most likely to require directions for traversing "familiar" routes.

Such differences in people's "social space" bear crucially on the question of what space a person may rightly occupy and what space he may not. The dimensions of one's social space vary from person to person and reflect each one's perception of his relationship to spatiality, some degree of which is determined culturally. Encounters between people of different spatial perceptions may lead to serious misunderstandings. Whereas some people may not like your trespassing on their territory, others may take little notice, and still other people may show no concern whatever about trespassing on the territory of *other* people.

Recognizing that differences exist in everyone's perceptions of space can play an enormous part in one's everyday experience. I was told by a famous Anglo-Catholic priest, who used to lecture at my school when I was a boy, that well-to-do people made the great mistake of supposing that poor people's "very, very horrid homes" were a result of their being *depraved*, not *deprived*. But if you looked at the behavior of the poor as depravity, he said, their acquisition of better living accommodations could not be expected to induce them to make a strong effort to maintain their homes well. In fact, however, they usually did *their level best* to maintain their homes well. Nevertheless, there was a tendency among rich people some forty years or so ago to "excuse" the wretched conditions under which very poor people had to live on the theory that poor people really *"liked* living that way." This is an error frequently made even today.

In addition to physical, cultural, and social differences in the ways in which people perceive time and space, there are personality differences. As noted in Chapter 3 concerning the Typology, a person who combines the functions of Sensation and Thinking (e.g., President Nixon) has characteristics that tend to limit his world, making him a rather territorial being. The combination of Intuition and Feeling—exemplified by Leo Tolstoy—tends to create an open-ended, expansive view of the world. The more one responds to both temporal and conceptual boundaries, the more likely one is to wish for a sharp definition of the space one occupies; the less one responds, the more nearly irrelevant temporal and conceptual boundaries become. A Feeling person's awareness of spatiality is more a reflection of his consciousness of the role of space in social affairs than it is of a perceived constraint or territorial limit on his own particular view of the world. His secondary function, if it is Sensation, can modify that spatial outlook and shift it toward the territorial end of the spectrum. Thus, one would suppose that, on the whole, people with a strong Sensation function and a strong secondary Feeling function would, if they are Extraverted, want a nice, large space. Extraverted Sensation-Feeling-type Lyndon B. Johnson made it well known that he liked nice large spaces.

From a typological point of view, space is important as a matter of how much of it a person feels he needs, of how much he understands about the amount of space other people need, and of what respect people give to each other's space and spatial needs.

Spatial Requirements for Well-Being

AN ANIMAL'S TERRITORY

There is solid biological—*ethological*—precedence for our attitudes toward space. As Dr. H. Hediger, director of Zurich Zoological Parks, showed many years ago, animals will not survive unless the spatial configurations of their surroundings are suitable for them. A particular sort of space, he observed, is essential for an animal's well-being. Certain animals must have a den or place of maximum security. If they are not allowed to have their proper retreat, they die. They must also possess a vantage point from which they can peer out over their territory, or smell out into their territory, depending upon which sense organ they favor.

Dr. Hediger also showed that you can produce the *functional equivalent of territory* if you know what you are about. The example he gave was the zebra, though the same could be said for bears. If the zebra is provided with a place where it can run and wear down its hoofs, a place where it can rub itself, and a place where it can urinate and defecate, it will remain remarkably healthy and hardy, even though the space does not seem at all to resemble the high veldt on which it lives in the wild. The space may even be highly constricted, forcing the zebra to run around in circles. But it doesn't seem to worry about this. Its hoofs get ground, and it remains in good health (provided that certain problems of parasites are looked after, but this is not truly a question of space). If the functional equivalent of a territory is not provided, however, the zebra's hoofs overgrow, and it becomes unable to run. Its skin, without a rubbing place, loses gloss and sometimes becomes infested with parasites. Without a familiar place for urinating and defecating, the zebra becomes uncomfortable—and probably will die.

All this concerns the idea of a biologically functional equivalent of space, or territory. Henri Bergson, the great French philosopher, pointed out long ago that mankind is a species that spends its early life in very small groups, and therefore human beings may be thought of functionally as creatures of small groups. They are also creatures with a very long childhood, a childhood that is spent crucially in the mother-child (or a mother surrogate and child) relationship. The child will be distressed if he cannot be, first, in tactile contact with his mother and, later on, at least in visual contact with her. This early experience makes children truly spatial—territorial—animals.

SPATIAL NEEDS OF CHILDREN

Hediger showed the early spatiality of human beings in another way. One of his zoologists visited some refugee children housed in a large building in Switzerland. The children were miserable in their cavernous surroundings. Hediger suggested that the space in the building be broken up and redesigned so that the children would have many corners and other discretely identifiable places. After room dividers were installed, the behavior of the children altered dramatically for the better, demonstrating beautifully that young humans are truly spatial animals.

From the beginning, the baby at his mother's breast creates his own space—presumably from his tactile, semivisual, and olfactory senses. He gradually enlarges his world. It soon includes his mother's head, then his bassinet area, and then parts of the environment beyond as he begins to crawl about. Bits of this space become very familiar, comfortable, and secure for him. When two of our three children—Julian and Fee—were very little, they had a tiny "house," which was three walls put against a fourth. Even though the house was quite open, the children loved to get inside and pretend that their parents couldn't get in. Julian, when he became upset, used to crawl under his bed and shout, "Keep out!," particularly if his feelings had been hurt or his pride trampled upon. (Perhaps I should add that Julian combines Sensation and Thinking functions, both of them territorial; Fee combines Sensation and Feeling, garnering for her the description the "velvet steam roller.") It is quite clear that it can make a considerable difference to children if their parents are able to provide them with appropriate spaces of their own. Many parents know this, and they do it. But sometimes parents do not understand how important appropriate spaces can be to the child, or cannot afford the room, and the child suffers in consequence.

All children seem to require a very dependable relationship with their mother or mother surrogate. How can this be brought about if the mother isn't able to relieve the pressure of mothering and "get away from it all" now and then? Surely, a child underfoot all day long will tend to make the mother irritable, and the mother-child relationship is bound to suffer. If, on the other hand, the mother will not let the child out of her sight for fear it will fall down the elevator shaft or be run over in the street, the relationship will also suffer, doubly from the child's viewpoint. What can be done to strike the middle ground? Clearly, the solution requires the availability of safe places for children to play. Many major metropolitan areas are already in serious trouble because they are building up into the air and are failing to provide ample safe play spaces for children. The problem is all the worse because *miles* of yesterday's play areas have been lost to the automobile with many serious—and some surprising—effects upon children and our evolving society.

Years ago mothers would let their little boys play in the streets. The bigger boys would be out on the periphery of the play neighborhood, and the little ones—just like little baboons —would be in the center of the "territory," not far from their homes, into which they could scuttle if danger threatened. Mothers didn't worry very much because they usually had older children look after the littler ones. Within the territory, the children played ball games, now and then dodging horses and making little excursions a short space outside the territory. Little boys, being territorial animals, rarely fought seriously, although they played at fighting a lot. As they returned from forays and extraterritorial excursions, they "got bigger" and their opponents "got smaller," and fights were usually called off. The nature of their combat was basically symbolic; you shouted insults when you were safely in your territory, near your home. Children gained a good deal of firsthand experience with "life" —in field conditions, so to speak—and they profited greatly from this opportunity.

The automobile changed everything. Children cannot dodge cars as well as they could dodge horses, and automobile drivers cannot tolerate additional distractions from children darting about the streets. The streets are lost as playgrounds, and the effects of the loss may be greater than seems immediately apparent.

Remaining in the street to play "chicken" with Fords and Chevrolets are only the fiercest boys. Does this loss of play space in which to give vent to childhood tendencies for territorial experience affect girls, too? Apparently not directly, for girls do not seem to need territories as much as the male animals do. There is a good deal of evidence, particularly among primates, that the territorial function is maintained largely by the males. One would suppose that this happens, in part, at least, because the females devote themselves to the vitally important biological activity of looking after and nurturing the young. There may be a quite unexpected effect upon girls, however, as a consequence of the high status achieved by the ferocious boys who dominate the scene. Girls sensitive to status are bound to admire the fierce males and choose them over others.

Automobile domination of city streets has thus produced a situation in which a boy's fierceness is seen as attractive—and probably sexually so—to girls. Through folly, the stratum of modern Western society that used to enjoy freedom to play in the streets may be shifting toward a whole new social configuration. But there are no signs that this possibility is recognized or that any actions are in the offing which would avert it.

Playgrounds and play areas may seem an extravagant use of valuable city space, but they are badly needed. Children must be able to play *together* if they are to share experiences and demonstrate to each other—and to adults—their innate lack of prejudice. Cities must design for this social need. There is no point in saying this space cannot be afforded. We might as well say we are going to send men on a rocket to the moon but can afford to put aboard an oxygen system adequate for only a one-way trip. If we decide we cannot afford play areas for our children, we will, in effect, be building "one-way cities."

It is interesting to consider where one-way cities would probably take us. If money is not spent for the allocation and development of adequate, appropriate spaces in cities for children to play in safely, then at least the same amount of money, if not more, will probably have to be spent for expanding the police force. Should this course be taken, there is little doubt that the basic configuration of the society will change further and move, by necessity if not design, toward a police state.

SPACE FOR THE SICK

When I was transferred to Malta, a British base in the Mediterranean, I had an opportunity to organize a working space and have a very educative experience. I was designing a small naval hospital there when an architect from England came in as a technical adviser. I showed him what I had in mind, and he told me to put away my pencils and protractors and simply explain to him *what it was I wanted to do in the place*. The marvelous simplicity of this approach to my problem was one of the most valuable lessons I've ever had! Although I had worked a short time in a surveyor's office, by no stretch of the imagination was I an architect, nor did I have any propensities for architecture. My proper function, obviously, was to think through what the space would be used for. This is much more difficult than one might suppose; it is easier to draw plans on paper than to work out exactly what will go on in a particular structure.

In 1950, toward the end of my senior psychiatric residency at

St. George's, in London, my colleague John Smythies and I began developing a theory of schizophrenia. I decided that I would like to work where I would have the opportunity to see a great many schizophrenics. At about this time, my wife noted in the London *Times* an advertisement appealing for psychiatrists in Saskatchewan, Canada, and she suggested I apply. I did so, and at Canada House, in London, I met a very interesting man, the late Griffith McKerracher, then director of Psychiatric Services for the Province of Saskatchewan, and later professor of psychiatry at the University of Saskatchewan. He painted an awfully gloomy picture of the psychiatric hospital in Saskatchewan. Nevertheless, I considered that at least a thousand schizophrenics would be my personal responsibility. Dr. Smythies, C. B. Ireland Professor of Psychiatric Research and Biochemistry at the University of Alabama, and I were working diligently on our general theory of schizophrenia. I felt that while there is a great deal to be said for general theorizing, there is also a great deal to be said for seeing the objects of one's theories. I moved to Saskatchewan.

It turned out that McKerracher had in no way exaggerated the problems at the Saskatchewan Hospital, in Weyburn. Physically, it was a minotaur's maze. You could get lost in it quite easily, and one full floor of the huge building was semi-underground. It was about a mile and a half around the eaves, a vast building on the Canadian prairie. Inside the hospital were nearly two thousand mentally ill people, most of them housed under the most dismal conditions. A building of its size should have accommodated with fair comfort about five hundred people— as it does today. But the space was designed to be a storehouse for human beings. With its vast dormitories, the hospital was hardly a suitable place for the mentally ill. The poor patients, in addition to all of this, were degraded, naked, and dirty. Some of them were obviously dying. All of them were being made sicker by their environment.

The hospital was what we would now call a "sociofugal" building—one whose design tends to discourage the occurrence of social relationships and to break them down when they do occur. Most railroad stations are excellent examples of sociofugality and quite correctly so, because it is not their function to encourage warm, close, sustained human relationships. Quite the contrary. One wants people to get on the trains and be about their business.

The hospital's enormous corridors produced visual distortions in photographs taken in them. The unfortunate patients with their own perceptual distortions would crouch, terrified, against the walls (very much as I crouched against the walls of the hospital in London just after my cataract operation because my new glasses had made it difficult to determine just where I was). The patients were particularly miserable in their huge dormitories and dayrooms; sometimes a hundred of them—unclothed —would be milling around, as in a concentration camp.

The first thing I had to do, as clinical director of the hospital, was to gain the confidence of the staff. The next thing was to show I was serious about doing something to correct the patients' situation. We were first faced with the problem of rehabilitating the hospital—breaking up spaces, getting the patients rehumanized, returning as many to normal life as we could. In doing this, we ended up developing new architectural theories.

Strange as it may seem, there were not at that time (1953) *any* architectural theories that accounted for the effects of space on behavior. There was a great deal of architectural chitchat about high-blown matters of aesthetics, but such down-to-earth matters as what a building might do to mad people were seldom, if ever, taken into account.

The first thing we did was to end the building's stench. We also made it look neat and clean and tidy. We installed more furniture. Furniture is always important because it defines space, and defining space means creating people-places, such as areas for sitting alone or in small groups. To make even the unalterably bad space less disturbing, we made it *identifiable*, painting the walls bright, cheerful, and often contrasting colors—instead of the institutional cream and green—so that patients could orient themselves more easily.

Once the changes had begun and were clearly going to continue, a shift started to develop in the staff's attitude. Our nurses began to grow hostile toward the notion of *not* doing something about the place, of simply leaving things alone. As time passed, this made it easier and easier to make changes, from administration and budgeting to space allocation.

Then Kyo Izumi, an architect friend of mine who had been living with his family in Regina, Saskatchewan, came to the hospital. Kyo had a brilliant training in architecture, having been a student at MIT, the Royal Institute of British Architects, and, I believe, briefly at Princeton. He walked around the hospital under the influence of LSD to simulate the perceptual responses of the schizophrenic inmates. This was the start of our work together; it led to several theoretical papers dealing with the effects of various sorts of space on sick people and what forms would be best and worst for them.

We observed that sick people, like well people, tend to want to withdraw physically from situations that are intolerable to them. If they cannot withdraw physically, they usually withdraw psychologically. We didn't want our sick people to withdraw psychologically; they were already psychologically withdrawn enough. We reckoned that the hospital, up to the time of our intervention, had been a machine for making patients withdraw psychologically instead of physically, for they had no place to go to be alone. We asked ourselves how we could achieve the conditions we wanted. In other words, *how do you build a better mental hospital?*

Using the lesson I had learned from the architect in Malta,

we began by specifying exactly what was to be done in the hospital space and what effects we wanted the space to achieve. The overriding constraint we wished to impose upon the design of space was Florence Nightingale's first principle for a hospital: to do the sick no harm—"Nothing unless good." How does one "do no harm" to a sick person with severe perceptual disorders?

It is obvious that the mentally ill need a space under their own control. If the space seems distorted to a patient—suddenly or constantly—he should be able to put out his hands and re-orient himself by reinforcing one sense modality (sight) with another (touch). The mentally ill also need a space that is aesthetically pleasing—a *nice* space, one they *want* to be in and which won't feel like a prison to them. And they need a modicum, at least, of comfort. Finally, they need to have a space that makes it clear where people are and who they are. Instead of milling around in a crowd of patients, they need to be with a few patients whom they can get to know—but only a few, not a lot.

We based our estimate of optimum group size for our patient population on the number of relationships the brain can handle when it is well; we reasoned that one would probably not be able to handle more when ill. That number is George A. Miller's "magic number" of seven plus or minus two, which comes to a group of five to nine (or six to ten, counting the first person).[1]

Only psychiatrists believe that they can handle "small" groups of fifteen to twenty people. Hostesses at dinner parties, diplomats, and even the British navy all recognize that the most cohesive, coherent grouping is not, ever, less than four or more than ten or eleven individuals. A sick person is clearly better off in a group of four than in a group of eight or ten; we settled

1. George A. Miller, "The Magic Number Seven, Plus-or-Minus Two: Some Limits on Our Capacity for Processing Information." *Psychological Review*, Vol. 63, No. 2 (March 1956), pp. 81–97.

for groups of four. Each member of a group was to have a small room of his own, his personal space, which would open onto a slightly larger space to be shared with the three other people. This slightly larger space for the face-to-face group then opened onto a still larger social area shared by the other members of the ward, who might be sixteen, twenty-four, twenty-eight, or even thirty-two people. While we preferred the smaller wards, for administrative reasons, it was sometimes considered necessary to have this social space sufficiently large for as many as eight groups of four to use it. This concept was developed into a wardlike configuration which would allow the hospital staff, situated in the center of the ward, to reach patients in their individual rooms or in their group rooms without great difficulty. It also made certain that the patients had no difficulty in finding their way to the nurses' station and did not get lost in those terrifying corridors found in so many mental hospitals. This particular structure was never built in our hospital in Weyburn, but variations of it have been built in Philadelphia, Washington, New York, Toronto, and elsewhere; indeed, every six months or so I hear of a new one going up. Kyo Izumi's Yorktown Hospital in Saskatchewan, which was completed in 1964, is widely acknowledged to be one of the best-designed mental hospitals in the world, even though, as we have since both agreed, it is not the hospital that we would like to design. Perhaps that will come sometime in the future.

Central to our planning was the importance of providing the patient with space to call his own. The worst kind of space is one in which the person has a vast area and nowhere specific to go. The big building that housed refugee children in Switzerland was simply a big building; no one could tell a child, "That's *your* space, but *this* is someone else's." We had much the same problem in the Saskatchewan hospital because we lacked the precise kind of space we needed to carry out our plan. We did have so-called seclusion rooms, however. There, patients whom the staff didn't like used to be locked up for an indefinite period—a very stupid idea.

We arranged for the seclusion rooms to be cleaned and smartened. Then, a patient who wished to have the privilege of being on his own—which was a considerable privilege in that badly designed place—was allowed to go and spend an hour or two or three in a room by himself.

The patients' reaction to this new practice was best demonstrated by one who was very keen on having one of those rooms for her own. We didn't have enough seclusion rooms to provide one for every patient who wanted a private place. We decided, however, to see how badly this particular patient wanted her own space by seeing how much she would pay for it. She had a tiny income—about three dollars a week—which we banked for her, though she didn't know this. We told her that the hospital could not afford to provide single rooms without extra charge and that she would have to pay for one if she wanted it. The "rent" started out at a quarter a week. A little while later, we told her that costs were rising and we would have to raise her rent to fifty cents a week. She agreed to the increase. But we kept raising the rent until the poor lady's total income was being "spent" on the room, or so she thought. We then told her we would have to raise the rent once more—which would have consumed more than her total income—and asked her how she was going to pay. She said, "I guess I'll just have to go out and get a job" (which, of course, was out of the question at that particular time). Apparently her space was so valuable to her that she would pay her all for it. She was much relieved when we told her that new circumstances made the "rent increase" unnecessary, and she was therefore relieved of the necessity of finding employment immediately.

We found evidence with other patients, as well, of the preciousness of personal space. When patients were very upset, they were delighted to be able to stay on their own in one of the well-appointed seclusion rooms until they felt better. This turned out to be very valuable *treatment,* in fact, for we noted decided improvement in several of the patients who had been accorded the privilege of privacy.

The "sanctuary" concept certainly wasn't new. A basic rule of many great monasteries was that every monk or nun should have a cell of his or her own. The idea was that one could do one's duty to God only on one's own. Perhaps you can do your duty to yourself only on your own sometimes, too. When you are ill, you have duties to your sick condition which are best performed in secluded repose. The failure to provide sick persons with the chance to be alone is a great mistake. It may also be an expensive one. The time spent in hospitals might be reduced by making private spaces available to patients when they need them, even if there are places for only *occasional seclusion.*

Principles for the Architecture of Human Space

From our experience with the Saskatchewan mental hospital, we developed three general principles for the architecture of human space.

The first is to determine *who* is going to be in the space and *what* they are going to do in it. That is, what are the legitimate and ethical goals of the social occupation and configuration of the space? It is actually quite revolutionary, architecturally, not to start at the other end—with a building (or, as it is in some cases, a monument to a benefactor, political leader, or the architect)—but instead to start at the *beginning,* with a social relationship that the building's design is supposed to facilitate.

The second principle: The architect must relate social purpose and function to spaces of an appropriate type. There are many instances in which this has not been done, perhaps the most incredible being a spiral staircase found in one institution for the blind. This would naturally have the effect of disorienting them. Equally damaging, though less obviously so, was an institution for the blind in Saskatchewan. The architect curved most of the surfaces, believing that this would prevent blind people from hurting themselves. Since they find their way about by learning patterns based upon the straight edges of walls, the blind were completely disoriented by this kindly intention.

The architect must also execute the third principle: Incorporate the spaces into a shape of an appropriate kind, which actually becomes the building.

Izumi applied these principles to the design of a building for a cooperative college that didn't have much money but did have a particular functional need in the building it wanted constructed. The administrators wanted a motel-type structure that would contain living accommodations for college members and would also facilitate interactions among them. Izumi found that a circular structure with centralized living quarters could be built within the college's budget. He arrived at this configuration by approaching the design problem from a standpoint opposite to the one used in the design of the mental hospital. There we wanted patients to socialize as they wished, to be able to withdraw physically when they wanted, to be able to call for the help of nurses when they wanted, and to know exactly how to find their way about under the burden of their distorted worlds. In the college building, the students were presumably well, and the college administration wanted them merely to socialize as quickly and as much as possible.

Izumi designed a circular building with the individual bedrooms arranged on the periphery, while in the center, lighted from above, was a sunken living space in which comfortable furniture was placed so that the students could not possibly avoid meeting each other. This was a highly sociopetal building fostering social relationships. The result: very rapid socialization at low cost. Moreover, the college received more money for its building fund because the environment created by the new building became increasingly popular and attracted more and more students. Increased income was wisely earmarked for construction of new buildings, but, not so wisely, the administration called at first for the old, linear-style building. The working staff objected, arguing that the new circular building saved a great deal of time in getting people to know one another. And, after all, wasn't that the point?

These hospital and college experiences suggest that one should impose different architectural criteria on structures used for different purposes. The object of the space in a railroad station, bus terminal, or airport is not principally to foster friendly relationships. Only small regions are required for that purpose, but it would appear at least reasonable to design places in terminals for people to wait in comfort and to greet and bid farewell to others. People space also should not include in it strange distortions that make people anxious and upset. Finally, a person unfamiliar with the building should be able to find his way easily about.

Unfortunately, often none of these criteria is met. The Trans World Airlines terminal at Kennedy Airport in New York is built rather like a gigantic two-legged octopus, with queer, humped, oval-shaped tunnels emanating from a globular center. These arms are, in fact, distorting machines—one cannot tell distance in them at all well.

Disorientation of that sort is the *last* thing you want to experience when you are rushing for a plane; nor is it particularly pleasing when you come off a flight, tired and perhaps already a little confused. In many passenger terminal buildings, there is almost no place where you can greet or say goodbye to anyone. O'Hare Airport in Chicago is a good example of this failure. At Dulles Airport in the United States capital, you are confronted by vast heights that make you feel you are in some sort of cathedral; the overall structure of the building looks like a huge Viking boat that somehow ran aground outside Washington. All of these architectural people-problems develop when designers start the wrong way around. An airport obviously has certain very legitimate sociofugal functions, moving people on their way to and from other places. But if people are going to stay there for any time at all, accommodations must be made. Yet most travel terminals are "ahuman" buildings, places where people wouldn't *want* to linger, although often they must. They become disaster areas for passengers stranded during bad weather.

Marshall McLuhan has developed a vision of a "global village" in which everyone on Earth has the opportunity to be in contact with each other by electronic means. While some people rejoice in this possibility, there are many who find it nightmarish. They may reject the concept partly on grounds of Introversion, for the person who lives within himself does not cotton to the notion of other people's butting in and disturbing his reflections continually.

But people could also reject a global-village view of the world on grounds of territoriality; the idea that the whole world would have access to them does not seem likely to inspire territorial people with a sense of warm involvement in affairs of the species. Rather, the "promise" of such involvement—and on a global scale, no less—would be more likely to pervade them with a sense of horror over the dreadful possibility that intrusion into their space was being made inevitable and beyond their control. The concept of a global village—everyone living and communicating in a seamless web of collapsed space and time— does not seem strange coming from McLuhan, who seems to combine the expansive Intuition and Feeling functions.

If we propose to survive, to improve ourselves and to develop our potentials, we shall want to build spaces suitable for human use and occupancy. If we do *not* propose to survive, or if we propose to make life hardly worth living, we shall probably simply move in the direction of trying to *adapt ourselves to our spaces*—as we seem mostly to be doing now—instead of *making spaces suitable for us*. It is as simple as that. Cities are places where *people* live, work, and play. Cities must be designed for actual, living members of our species, not for hypothetical beings. Is it not extraordinary that most of the buildings in a city look as though they might well have been built for some other species or for some other purpose than to facilitate the social functioning of humans?

What can be said about designing city buildings is best illustrated in our experience with the design of the Saskatchewan mental hospital. According to the principles of socioarchitecture, if we want to economize on space, the pressure should be applied economically, *not* to the *quality* of space but to the *quantity* of space. In our many travels across Canada by railroad, my family (four at the time) found that we could travel relatively comfortably in a space of about six feet by six feet by six feet. If worse comes to worst, a mentally ill person can probably put up with just this small space, *as long as it is properly equipped*. Yet governments do not seem to understand these things. They continue to put up (and put up with) enormous buildings that torture people. They do not *mean* to torture us, of course. But they do so, nevertheless, by constructing buildings that do not meet human needs.

While the principles of effective, humane design and utilization of space seem relatively simple to understand, the *practice* of the principles seems to be difficult. It is like $E = mc^2$. You can easily grasp Einstein's brilliant mathematical formulation in a theoretical sense; it is a long haul from there, though, to the development of a nuclear reactor and a nuclear bomb. Without Einstein's basic principle, the notion of *any* sort of nuclear energy device would not even occur to you because you would not know where to look for technical guidance.

At least we now know where to look for many of the crucial criteria in the human use of space. That is, in most cases, it is relatively easy to say what is needed to design a contained space properly for human occupancy and use. And when we are not certain about what is needed we can apply a few simple principles and find out.

5

The Special Worlds
of Madness

The Prevalence of Schizophrenia

Strange as it may seem, understanding another person's world is often easier if he is mad.

The reason for this is that what the mad person communicates is often so deeply disturbing that even the most insensitive person is made aware of the oddness—the *distinctiveness*—of the madman's world. Nevertheless, as odd to us sane people as the mad person's perceived world might seem from his description of it, *his world is every bit as real to him as our worlds are to us.* Indeed, a good deal of the behavior of mentally ill people is probably very much the way ours would be if we were in their place. But we are not in their place, and we have to make a special effort to understand them.

Suppose, for example, someone told you that he felt as if he were turning to stone (which is not an uncommon experience in schizophrenia) *and* that he wished to die so that he could be released from the stony feelings of lifelessness. The otherwise incomprehensible death wish should be completely comprehensible to anyone who can understand that another person, as a consequence of severe mental illness, may actually experience the almost inexpressibly horrible feeling of turning to stone. Who *wouldn't* want to die under such circumstances?

Experience with schizophrenia's "worlds of madness" can be exceedingly useful in understanding more normative worlds. A person's self-world *changes* when he becomes mentally ill, very much the way a person's world changes under the influence of psychedelic or narcotic drugs. Such changes—natural or drug-induced—are often expressed as alterations in mind and behavior. People experiencing these changes may sometimes be cheery, or depressed and frightened. Just as a mutation in an organism is a "marker" that reveals the existence of a particular altered gene in that organism, a marked change in mood or behavior indicates the existence of a particular aspect of a person's inner world, be it normal or not.

A person's perceptions of himself and of others shape and shade the range of roles he plays in life. If a mentally ill person sees himself as the creator of the universe, for instance, he may decide to assume no role at all in life, believing either that he has already taken all possible roles or that playing any role in society would be a mere trivialization of himself. The variety and degree of change in one's self-world that is brought about by madness or drugs sometimes almost defy description. How, for example, can a person possibly convey the experience of losing dimensionality and/or feeling as though he has become a "point without time"?

Another way of phrasing that question is to ask what it is really like to be mad. The answer, sadly, is shared excruciatingly by an enormous number of people all over the world who inhabit their own special worlds of madness. It has been estimated that *at least two out of every hundred persons on Earth* suffer from schizophrenia in some form or degree. The disease knows no national or cultural boundaries and responds to no quarantine or immunization. When Emil Kraepelin, the psychiatrist, took a trip around the world in the 1890s, he came back tremendously pleased to find that people suffered from dementia praecox (the old name for schizophrenia) in all cultures; indeed, a psychiatrist who cannot even talk a patient's language can often diagnose schizophrenia with the help of an interpreter. It is probably not too much to say that the universality of this disease is one of the most human things about human beings.

Yet each person's madness is unique—for him alone—and this has been one source of difficulty in formulating a sound theory of schizophrenia. The reason, it seems, is that often there is an almost infinite variety of variables in the perceptual sphere that become affected in schizophrenia and through which the schizophrenic receives the data of his special world. This makes the psychiatrist's task hopelessly unmanageable without some sort of objective *measure*.

Suppose that I am having interesting disturbances in color perception—hallucinations. And suppose also that you are experiencing disturbances in the way you perceive your body— hallucinations, too, but of a different sort. You may say you have the extraordinary feeling that you are being turned to stone. Since this is demonstrably (to me) *not* happening, I may be tempted to conclude that you are mad and that such hallucinatory feelings and thoughts are the essence of madness. On the other hand, I may think that the radiant colors I am seeing all about me are the heavens opening up for me. Similarly, you may conclude that I am mad and that *this* sort of vagrant vision and the accompanying sensations and thoughts that you do not share are what constitute madness.

Neither of us would think himself mad, and each of us would think the *other* mad. This tragic situation actually occurs quite frequently in mental hospitals; patients will often demand to know why they are being shut up "with all these lunatics." It may seem at first a hard thing to do, but I have found it very important to convince the patient that he indeed *is* mentally ill, while at the same time explaining to him that, of course, efforts are being made to make him well again.

To appreciate more fully the predicament in which the mentally ill person finds himself, consider how our ability to function in our day-to-day lives depends upon the clarity and constancy of our perceptions and upon their correspondence, roughly, to the perceptions of other people in our environment. If these capabilities become interfered with, you will, in a sense, become a foreigner in your own country. A society spends a good deal of time, money, and energy in teaching its members the various behavioral "signals" that are appropriate to that society. If your sense of time and space is disordered, or if you see signals that no one else sees, your behavior—appropriate, perhaps, in the context of your distorted world—sets you off on the road first to alienation and then to expulsion from society as a misfit. A certain amount of conformity is required from all of us. In order to conform, one must be able to recognize the signals to conform to. Conforming to signals that are *not* shared by the rest of society simply won't work.

Part of the problem concerns what one means by thinking and feeling "normally." Paranoid people—schizophrenic or not —often think clearly; the key is that they think (as, for instance, Wilhelm Reich thought) with data that are not shared by the rest of us. A brief example: Reich, a one-time psychoanalyst, apparently "saw" a certain "blue halo" surrounding dead fish (no one else could see it). It appears that on the basis of this unshared data, he built his theory of the orgone, a particular kind of biological energy. Although other people practically never shared his remarkable experience, Reich had a personality that was so forceful that he was able to persuade a good many that their inability to see what he saw was all the worse for *them.*

Many mental patients have disturbances in sense perception that they reasonably *suppose* are shared by others. They are frequently surprised and sometimes incredulous to discover that this is not so. My experience in these matters has led me to conclude that it is utterly impossible for one to judge the quality of a person's thinking without knowing the nature of the data on which his thinking is based.

The question of feeling takes a similar shape. How can one possibly determine what a person is feeling, and whether or not it is "appropriate"? Suppose one sees a world full of pain, bitter irony, and distress; this might lead him to laugh bitterly at the irony, or to cry over the pain, or to do both at once. Is such behavior "appropriate"? We see perfectly normal people do this sort of thing in the midst of great stress, say, from some calamitous event—war, earthquake, or flood—and we accept it straightaway. Groups of people reacting to a catastrophic occurrence might include some who are dancing and singing in the street, others who are weeping or frozen in horror or catatonic—and we "understand." What differentiates such behavior from utter madness?

"Insanity": Severe Disturbance of Sense Perception

In the mid-nineteenth century, the term "insanity" referred to a specific mental illness described in John Conolly's Croonian Lectures of 1849 and in his famous book *Inquiry Concerning the Indications of Insanity*. (Dr. Conolly, of Hanwell, London, was one of the greatest psychiatrists of his time. Earlier, in 1758, Dr. William Battie, a notable and civilized eighteenth-century physician, had written his famous *Treatise on Madness* and advocated humane treatment and well-designed buildings for the mentally ill. Battie was one of the first men to introduce postgraduate study of psychiatric illness—madness—and his views survived his death for many years.) Insanity was seen by Conolly as, in essence, a disturbance of sense perception so severe that "comparing power" had been lost; today, we would probably use the term—which is no better—"reality testing."

However, severe perceptual disturbances that interfere with one's ability to discriminate the real from the unreal are not what is meant by "insanity" today. The word "insanity" has largely lost its *medical* meaning for a social one. "Insanity" is now used when a person is deemed not only lacking in responsibility for self-care and care of others but is also dangerous to himself and others. Under this "definition," society has only two courses of action: expulsion from the community or incarceration in the community, which constitutes expulsion from the normal operations of the community, anyway.

The kind of psychosis that is most widespread in the world —schizophrenia, as it is now called—was described by Conolly in the mid-nineteenth century, by Battie a hundred years earlier, and by Thomas Willis, the father of modern neurology, a hundred years before Battie. Each of them characterized the illness as a disturbance in sense perception. Willis, in fact, described the sick brain as "distorted looking glasses that do not rightly collect images of things nor truly object them to the rational soul." (We might use the word "project" today, or perhaps "display.")

If the Willis-Battie-Conolly view was so sound, why is it not popular now? Oddly, it may be simply because modern man lacks personal experience with perceptual distortions to which people of the Conolly period were commonly exposed. Consider the following.

Conolly died in 1866. Lister's famous first paper on antisepsis was published two to three years later. That paper became the basis of modern surgical practice, and it initiated what grew to become a massive attack on infections of all kinds. Before then, many surgeons had taken the view that infection was a *good* thing; they eagerly looked for the presence of "laudable pus." During the century following Conolly's death, a host of drugs—antipyretics, analgesics, hypnotics, and antiseptics—was introduced. These were followed by techniques of immunization, antibiotics, the use of vitamins, blood transfusion, and other marvels. The steady, cumulative effect of these advances was to make the commonest source of perceptual anomalies—infection, usually with fever and delirium—less and less frequent.

Only within the last thirty years or so, in fact, has delirium become a somewhat unfamiliar event in everyday sickness. It used to be *expected* in illness, and up to about thirty-five years ago there were very few people who had not experienced one or more episodes of delirium. These were matters of universal experience about which no one had to be convinced.

Doctors, like everyone else, absorbed without realizing it the conventional wisdom of society at the time—changes in bodily status were frequently accompanied by changes in perceptions. No school of psychiatry seems to have doubted this until the 1930s at the very earliest. Partly in consequence, it seems, general psychiatrists, psychobiologists, and psychoanalysts—including the Jungians—all believed that schizophrenia was an organic disease in which some unknown toxin was elaborated, influencing the functioning of the brain. Karl Menninger in his first book, *The Human Mind* (published in 1930), wrote, "Schizophrenia is a long delirium."

From the 1940s on, however, psychiatry seems to have been far more impressed by the *differences* among the "toxic" states of mind than by their similarities. This was almost exactly the time when medical progress made many of these same toxic states more and more infrequent; when they did occur, they lasted shorter and shorter periods. Thus, few in an entire new generation of students and doctors had themselves experienced a sustained delirium, for even the first signs of such a condition usually led to vigorous and frequently successful efforts to prevent its occurrence.

Efforts to grasp the true nature of the bizarre ailments of the mind had been made more difficult at the turn of the century by Eugen Bleuler, a contemporary of Freud and Kraepelin. Bleuler coined the term "schizophrenia." He did not intend it to mean a splitting of personality but a *fragmenting* or *shattering* of the self into many pieces, terms that more closely describe the illness as it actually manifests itself. Freud played hardly any role at all in exploring and explaining the world of schizophrenia (he wasn't a trained psychiatrist). Jung's association test provided evidence that thinking was disordered in schizophrenia. But Bleuler maintained that the disease was the result of a *"slippage" in affect,* that is, a dislocation between thinking and feeling. He produced not one jot of evidence for his view; nevertheless, it became very popular as a result largely, I would guess, of simple boredom in the field and lack of a good theory.

One other contributor to the confusion over the nature of schizophrenia that has prevailed for more than half a century was Adolf Meyer, a notable and very influential Swiss-American psychiatrist, who in his later years was head of Phipps Clinic of Johns Hopkins University. It was Meyer's notion that schizophrenia stemmed from a "deterioration of habit." He felt that the loss of habits, which are slowly and laboriously formed, would gravely deform a person's world into that of the schizophrenic. This strange notion did not come to anything, but it did make matters rather worse for American psychiatry for a time.

What psychiatry was left with, after all the confusion, was the view that schizophrenia essentially constituted a profound disturbance ("slippage") in both thinking and feeling. Precisely *how* this disturbance was caused was (and still is) an open question. The answer will remain elusive as long as there is no way to *measure* objectively both the degree and the character of the disturbance. (I believe that my colleagues and I *have* now developed instruments for measuring the worlds of madness. These tools are described in Chapter 8.)

As a physician-psychiatrist who must constantly share other people's worlds, I would like to think of myself as being able to see the world through their eyes, but that would simply be a delusion. It appeared to me many years ago that to be of any real help to a patient, a physician had to be able to understand what was happening to the patient as the patient perceived it. Sources of information on how to do this seemed pitifully few, inadequate, and, for the most part, utterly unusable. My work with mentally ill people, my great good fortune of knowing and working with Aldous Huxley for ten years, and my work with psychedelic substances gradually led me to the idea that one's personal world might, under various circumstances, literally *change*. Moreover, on the basis of my own experiences with world-changing perceptual aberrations through psychedelics, it did not seem in the least bit unlikely that someone might get *stuck* in one of those "strange" worlds. Indeed, some strange worlds may not be strange at all to people who inhabit them as a consequence of alterations in perceptual coordinates, such as time and space; to them, "nonstrange" worlds would be the strange ones.

The Reality of the Madman's World—for the Madman

My first use of a psychedelic substance convinced me in ninety minutes flat that schizophrenic patients are not talking about "as if," hypothetical, or "unreal" experiences; *they are describing what is really happening to them.* I remember becoming fascinated, about an hour and a half after I had taken mescaline for the first time, by a piece of bluish-green wallpaper, then horrified when it started turning into the winter sea of the North

Atlantic where, in a desperate convoy battle in March 1943, I had been present on the bridge of a destroyer when two ships were sunk and, despite our best efforts, many men were lost. The mescaline seemed to have "eliminated time" for me, and I was being translated back to an earlier space. I recall that I felt strongly I did not want to go and that I diverted my attention from the wallpaper, terminating that particular hallucination. I was conscious, after all, that I was undertaking an experiment. But suppose I hadn't been able to recall that? Would I have been dragged back once more into that agonizing and deadly battle?

From that time on, it has been difficult for me not to accept the possibility that ordinary objects—window frames, table-cloths, doorknobs, etc.—may acquire very special significance for persons undergoing extraordinary perceptual experiences, as users of psychedelics and schizophrenics (and the delirious) often report.

Believing that it was extremely important to understand the experiences of my schizophrenic patients, I read many accounts of the illness and listened carefully to what my own patients told me. Still, the understanding I was able to achieve in this way was by no means equal to *experiencing*, firsthand as it were, a schizophrenic episode myself. This, of course, is almost impossible to do if you do not have the illness. I say "almost" deliberately. While there has been a great deal of argument as to whether people can experience a simulated schizophrenialike episode "artificially," distortions in one's experiential world that seem practically indistinguishable from those in schizophrenia can be achieved through the use of psychedelic drugs.

A "Psychedelic" (Chemical) Theory of Schizophrenia

In 1950, Dr. John Smythies and I, working together at St. George's Hospital in London, evolved a theory of schizophrenia in which psychedelic drugs were seen as related to substances that occur naturally in the body and whose metabolism may be involved in the production of the "psychedeliclike experiences" that schizophrenics endure in their distorted perceptual worlds.

Basically, we had observed that the molecular structure of mescaline closely resembles that of adrenaline. Inasmuch as the function of a substance is often related to its structure (very specifically so in the case of enzymes and hormones), we reasoned that the function of adrenaline, slightly altered through faulty metabolism, might resemble the psychedelic function of mescaline. In other words, the perceptual disturbances that schizophrenics suffer would presumably be caused by chemicals produced naturally, but abnormally, in their bodies.

The first two papers that Dr. Smythies, Dr. Abram Hoffer, and I wrote together, "Schizophrenia—A New Approach" (1952) and "Schizophrenia—A New Approach II" (1954), formed the basis for two different but related theories, one of which met with the severest disapproval initially from chemists and later from psychiatrists.

The first theory was that adrenaline could be what is known as "transmethylated" and thus turned into a mescalinelike compound. Dr. Smythies raised this possibility in May 1950. Professor John Harley Mason of the Department of Chemistry at the University of Cambridge agreed that it was possible, even though at that time this particular chemical process had not been demonstrated in the animal body.[1]

Two years later, Dr. Hoffer and I, after a series of experiments on ourselves and our brave wives, suggested that adrenochrome, an intermediate oxidation product of adrenaline (or something like it), might be the villain.

I tend to favor the adrenochrome hypothesis, though a mixture

1. This shows how the so-called "transmethylation" hypothesis of schizophrenia came into being. It is currently guiding research in many laboratories around the world.

of the two theories is wholly possible. There is strong evidence that adrenochrome produces effects that mimic schizophrenia in man and change the behavior of animals. There is also growing evidence that adrenochrome occurs naturally in the human body, and there is some—though no conclusive—evidence that more of it is present in schizophrenics than in other people.

Recent findings by four British doctors, B. C. Barrass and D. B. Coult, of the Chemical Defense Establishment, Porton Down, Salisbury, Wilshire, and A. C. Drysdale and Surgeon Commander Marjot, of the Royal Victoria Hospital, Netley, Southampton, Hampshire, suggest that there is a substance present in the urine of schizophrenics that might play some part in accelerating the production of adrenochromelike substances.

That adrenochrome does, in fact, induce psychosislike experiences was evident from my first experiments with it, which I recorded in part as follows:

After the purple red liquid was injected into my right forearm, I had a good deal of pain. . . . After about ten minutes, while I was lying on a couch looking up at the ceiling, I found that the ceiling had changed color. It seemed that the lighting had become brighter. . . . I closed my eyes and a brightly colored pattern of dots appeared . . . [which] gradually resolved themselves into fishlike shapes. I felt that I was at the bottom of the sea or in an aquarium among a shoal of brilliant fishes. . . . When I left [the laboratory], I found the corridors outside sinister and unfriendly. I wondered what the cracks in the floor meant and why there were so many of them. Once we got out of doors, the hospital buildings, which I know well, seemed sharp and unfamiliar. As we drove through the streets, the houses appeared to have some special meaning, but I couldn't tell what it was. In one window, I saw a lamp burning, and I was astonished by its grace and brilliance. I drew my friends' attention to it, but they were unimpressed. . . . I began to feel that I was losing touch with everything . . . I began to wonder whether I was a person any more and to think I might be a plant or a stone. As my feeling for these inanimate objects increased, my feeling for and my interest in humans diminished. I felt indifferent toward humans and had to curb myself from making unpleasant remarks about them. . . . Time seemed to be of no importance. . . . I [had] this "glass wall, other side of the barrier" feeling . . . fluctuant, almost intangible . . . but I [knew] it [was] there. . . .

Those and other experiences with adrenochrome clearly did not exclude the possibility that this substance was somehow involved in producing the odd experiences that schizophrenics endure, but neither did such experiments show that adrenochrome was, in fact, involved in the disease. Further evidence one way or the other might be obtained, we thought, if one were able to diminish the effects of adrenochrome *and* of psychedelic drug experiences *and* of schizophrenia's symptoms in some way, preferably chemically. This meant that one would want to select a substance that would interfere with the accumulation of adrenochrome in the body, and then see whether it would reduce the effects of injected adrenochrome, ingested mescaline, and the symptoms of schizophrenia.

The compound we selected for this was nicotinic acid, otherwise known as niacin or vitamin B_3. Chemically, it would accept methyl groups, and so interfere with the transmethylation of adrenaline to a mescalinelike substance, and would also interfere with adrenaline synthesis and thereby block adrenochrome production and accumulation.

Use of niacin—particularly in conjunction with ascorbic acid (vitamin C)—proved effective in reducing the perceptual disturbances generated by injected adrenochrome, ingested mescaline, and schizophrenia. Treatment of schizophrenic patients with niacin (or its amide, nicotinamide) began in 1952 and has met with some success over the years in the hands of many physicians.[2] The vitamin is administered orally in massive

2. Other physicians have not had the same success. Dr. Smythies considers that the design of the clinical trials used so far is inadequate because he and many others believe that schizophrenia is not a single disease. The position regarding niacin today is that some patients respond

doses. Three grams a day is the usual dosage, but daily administrations of as much as 12 grams have been used effectively against schizophrenia without untoward side effects.

The chief and most annoying "side effect" of large doses of niacin is transient, lasting only about an hour, and disappears altogether after about three days of the regimen. This is the heavy flushing that a person experiences shortly after taking his first large doses of the vitamin—say, half a gram or a gram after a meal. The person's complexion reddens; he feels hot and itches for a half hour or so. This is caused partly by dilation of blood vessels but mostly by the dumping into the tissues of histamines from body cells. The experience subsides with subsequent administrations of the vitamin because the histamine level in the body's cells gradually stabilizes at a low level, so that large amounts cannot be dumped suddenly into the system in response to niacin ingestion. Seen as an annoyance by many persons beginning to take niacin, flushing is probably a boon in disguise. A person usually finds that taking "medicine"—niacin is more properly a food or nutrient—to *prevent* a particular condition is hard to remember because the condition to be prevented is not present as a reminder, as an infection would remind one to take an antibiotic. In the case of niacin—which is taken preventively

---

very well, some are unchanged, and a small number may even be worsened somewhat. These results are probably partially due to the fact that schizophrenia is more than one illness with similar symptoms that result from quite different disease processes, some of which derive from inherent genetic differences. Also, conditions like anemia, high blood pressure, and pneumonia, which were once thought to be single illnesses, are now known to be many separate ones requiring wholly different treatment.

We already know that two of five chronic schizophrenics become iller when given 20 grams of the nutrient (amino acid) methionine, while three of five are none the worse. Some schizophrenics benefit greatly from a new drug, Pimozide, while others become iller. Dr. Carl C. Pfeiffer has shown that about 50 percent of schizophrenics have low blood histamine levels, 30 percent have normal, and 20 percent have very high levels; the low histamine cases respond favorably to niacin. Experimental design must take these known differences into account, and there are probably many other differences we cannot yet recognize.

by schizophrenics, alcoholics, coronary-prone individuals, and arthritics—one is given very good reason to remember to take the vitamin regularly. Failure to do so causes the person's histamines to build up again in his cells, and resumption of niacin use will produce the annoying flushing again.

Nicotinic acid, niacin, vitamin B₃, whatever you want to call it, is cheap, easily available without prescription, and safe, but its effects in massive doses touch on some of the most serious and difficult health problems facing us today.

Niacin lowers blood cholesterol (which has been associated with the development of atherosclerosis and heart attacks) and improves blood flow generally, particularly in tiny vessels such as those in the heart and brain. A group of 160 patients in Florida, each of whom had suffered one heart attack, received massive doses (3 grams a day) of niacin over a ten-year period. The usual actuarial recurrence figures forecast sixty-two deaths in that group over that period of time, but only six deaths actually occurred, a reduction of 90 percent. Niacin has now been used in the prophylactic treatment of heart conditions in well over a thousand cases with impressive success and is one of the three compounds tested by the National Institutes of Health in its study of coronary death prevention. (This effect of niacin should also reduce the likelihood of stroke.)

Arthritics also appear to benefit considerably from massive doses of niacine or the amide form of the vitamin, niacinamide. This effect—unexpected and still unexplained (niacin's influence on cell histamine levels may be involved)—was reported first in 1949 by Dr. William Kaufman, of Bridgeport, Connecticut. Experience since then has uniformly supported Dr. Kaufman's early assessment of niacinamide's beneficial effects on arthritis in several of its forms.

Niacin has been used with great effect also in the treatment of alcoholism and "bad trips" suffered by users of psychedelic drugs.

If niacin is so wonderful—showing merit in the treatment and/or prevention of several conditions for which there exists no other really effective treatment or prophylaxis today (schizophrenia, alcoholism, atherosclerosis, stroke, coronary disease, arthritis)—one wonders why it is not more widely used. At least some of the reasons are indicated in Dr. Kaufman's comments about the vitamin's failure to achieve wider acceptance in the treatment of arthritis despite his reports of its salutary effects on this enigmatic affliction. He wrote:

I think that two factors have made it difficult for doctors to accept the concept. . . . The first difficulty was the advent of cortisone (whose failure to achieve its initial promise in treatment of arthritis has been disappointing), and the second was the fact that my [massive] use of the vitamin was such a large departure from the recommended daily allowance for vitamins by the National Research Council.[3]

A liberal interpretation of Dr. Kaufman's view would thus hearken back to our old bugaboos: *conventional wisdom* and *establishmentarianism*. What would we do without them? What we *could* do without them!

3. William Kaufman, *Common Forms of Joint Disfunction*. Boston: E. W. Hildreth & Co., 1949.

6

The Special Worlds
of Drugs

Similarities to the Worlds of Madness

Although the world was sharper and brighter, it was also infinitely more fluid and changeable. A bird in the street, a sparrow, small and far away, might suddenly become the focus of one's attention, the most important thing in the world, the bird of the world, a key to the universe. Beauty, a "terrible beauty," was being born every moment. Phrases such as "I have seen with the eye of the world, the eye of the newborn, the eye of the new dead" sprang to my tongue apparently without construction. . . .

I also noticed that my hands tingled and I had a curious dirty feeling which seemed to be inside my skin. I scrutinized one hand, and it became shrunken and clawlike. I realized that beneath the withered, leathery skin was bone and dust alone—no flesh. . . .

I asked for some water . . . and found that it tasted strange. I wondered whether there might be something wrong with it; poison crossed my mind. . . . I looked into the glass of water. Its swirling depths were a vortex which went down into the center of the world and the heart of time. . . . Once on the street, the distortion of perspective became evident. The distances were immense. The colors vivid, the

August sun burned on a patch of willow herb . . . with such intensity that I had to shade my eyes. Everything was sharp as a painting by Vermeer. . . .

It was particularly difficult to get accustomed to changes in body image. At one moment, I would be a giant in a tiny cupboard, and the next, a dwarf in a huge hall. It is difficult enough to explain what it feels like to be Gulliver or Alice in Wonderland in the space of a few minutes, but it is nearly impossible to communicate an experience which amounts to being uncertain whether one was in Brobdingnag or Lilliput. . . .

[Unexpectedly, I was extremely sensitive] to other people's feelings toward me and toward each other . . . my friends' criticisms of me [gave me] *physical* discomfort. If they urged me to do something I did not want to do, it jarred, and this jarring was accompanied sometimes by a burning taste or smell. Most unexpected was my response to a slight difference of opinion between [them]. This was a minor affair due to one's wanting me to eat and [the other's] wanting me to discuss my experiences. . . . The room, which had been brilliantly lit, [appeared to] become dark. The colors lost some of their vitality, and I felt . . . criticism . . . as a bitter taste, an acrid smell and an ill-localized pain somewhere between my shoulder blades and my spine. All the time, my . . . companions were changing, sometimes with reference to what they were saying and doing and sometimes with reference to my inner experience. . . .

It is not hard to see that the above quotation resembles with remarkable fidelity some of the descriptions of perceptions and sensations experienced by people with serious mental illness. However, the foregoing remarks are *not* the remembered ravings of a lunatic, but a selection of passages from notes that I myself took of my own experience in 1951 following consumption of about 400 milligrams of pure high-quality mescaline provided by my colleague Dr. Smythies at his home in England.

Clearly, the distorted world of the schizophrenic bears a striking resemblance to the mescalinized person's changed world. It is little wonder, then, that drugs such as mescaline and the other hallucinogens have been referred to as "psychotomimetics," for their effects do, indeed, mimic psychoses. One might wonder, however, why anyone would want deliberately to undergo a period of drug-simulated insanity if madness is as distressing a state as persons who have experienced it spontaneously have said it is. Furthermore, to sample psychosis through drugs entails the very real risk—under certain circumstances—that one may become "stuck" for an indefinite period in an alien world of madness.

Man's Pursuit of Strange Experiences

I believe the answer lies in man's nature, partly as a drug- and medicine-taking animal and partly as a creature forever preoccupied with the desire to enjoy "strange experiences."

Potions containing substances that affect a person's state of mind were probably first brewed as a kind of beer that the caveman treated himself both to and with. People have eaten mind-affecting plant alkaloids—such as those found in mushrooms, nutmeg, morning glory seeds, and pine nuts—in both primitive and advanced societies throughout recorded history. Mind-affecting substances have long been used as medicine and for religious purposes—sometimes both at the same time. Their effects are altered states of consciousness: "changed worlds."

When men have not been gratifying their appetites for strange experiences with drugs—alcohol, opiates, and the milder hallucinogens—they have accomplished similar effects through ordeals, some of them quite repellent by the views of today's society. The Spartans employed flogging; some American Plains Indians worshiped the sun by hanging themselves by thongs through their deltoid muscles and twirling around. Severe physiological stress—which can be brought about through flagellation, laceration, exposure to fire or intense heat, or near-suffocation—

can cause the production of large quantities of histamines and adrenaline in the body, and these can lead to modifications in one's perceptual world.

Ordeals and drugs are not the only means for modifying one's experiential world. Some persons actually have a natural talent for controlling their experience without either outside aid (as from stress or drugs) or any internal influence (as from mental illness). Saint Ignatius Loyola selected the first Jesuits by the flexibility of their perceptions and their powers of imagery, according to the "Rule of Saint Ignatius." Taught to control their powerful imagery, the original Jesuits became "heroes of will and achievement." The Jesuit "empire" in South America and their other missionary activities reaching even to faraway China are illustrations of their extraordinary zeal and heroism. Saint Ignatius had observed that some people were not capable of imaging in their minds even a little piece of white paper, whereas others could imagine, if they wished, the most lovely harlot, or Jesus on the cross, in living color and three-dimensional detail. Through application of Saint Ignatius' Rule (in which their interest seems now to have waned), the Jesuits developed techniques involving use of their powerful imagery and keen perception of the world for controlling experience. This was their way of achieving the new and strange experiences that man seems destined forever to pursue.

Certain practices of the church for a very long time made these strange—"transcendental"—experiences accessible even to followers who did not have the knack of powerful imagery. Before the development of means for storing fresh foods over long periods, people underwent severe vitamin deficiencies during the winter and immediately thereafter experienced genuine vitamin starvation during Lent. The physiological effects of this stressful regimen often were augmented by illness in many forms, which was frequently accompanied by fever. Religious prescriptions, compounded in this way of severe physiological stress and hypertheological focus, greatly facilitated the achievement of profound religious experience among even the least adept at imagery.

The achievement of altered states of consciousness through the use of hallucinogenic chemicals, stressful ordeals, techniques for manipulating powerful imagery abilities, or devout adherence to stress-producing religious ritual does not explain *why* man yearns for strange experiences. To satisfy that yearning, he will punish and abuse himself physically, risk losing his mind, and —as Thomas Traherne, seventeenth-century mystic and poet, wrote—"put away the dirty devices of the world" in order to see things "as a little child again."

It may well be that mankind's yearning for strange experiences springs from a sort of pan-specific drive for both solidarity and distinction, for both belonging and not-belonging. It is this drive, it seems, that has led humanity on a quest that is exemplified today by the so-called drug culture. It is a quest for new worlds that are very different from the ordinary, where people can find answers to questions, both private and cosmic:

Who am I?

Why am I?

What is the meaning of life? Of love? Of death?

What is It all about?

Seeking answers to such questions has been the objective of the great religions and of some of the greatest humans who ever lived. The aim: to achieve a kind of total experience that affirms reality by penetrating to its very essence. Drug taking is only one way of pursuing that goal—a universal and timeless but also comparatively feeble way of pursuing a "really real reality" through the attainment of a sort of "cosmic consciousness." Great men and women have joined in this quest by a large variety of means throughout recorded history: Jesus went into the wilderness; Buddha sought his nirvana; Socrates seems to have been rendered immobile by his daimon. And poor William

Henley, suffering from tuberculosis among other things, pro-claimed:

> *Out of the night that covers me,*
> *Black as the Pit from pole to pole,*
> *I thank whatever gods may be*
> *For my unconquerable soul.*

The great saints did not lay claim to captaining their souls but in another way saw themselves aligned with God, as did Lady Juliana of Norwich, the famous anchorite, who expressed her sense of becoming Christ in what appears to me to have been a catatonic experience. Just as madmen, saints, and the drugged have told of seeking and sometimes finding transcendental experiences, persons of a decidedly more practical bent have done so, too—mathematicians, scientists, and even astronauts. Newton, Kepler, Alfred Russel Wallace, and Einstein are only a few of the examples to be found in the "real world" of science.

Such men were true visionaries, and inasmuch as visions are by definition unreal or "extrareal," attempts are usually made to respectabilize them. We do this by viewing the musings of great visionaries, in retrospect, as objects of legitimate preoccupation for respectable persons of the present. This is seldom so.

Sir Isaac Newton, the fruits of whose mathematical genius dominated Western scientific thought for well over two centuries, considered his finest work to be his interpretations of the biblical Book of Daniel, to which he devoted several million words in manuscript. Einstein is described in most history books as having been drawn toward the conceptualization of his famous relativity theories by his fascination as a young man with the Michaelson-Morley experiment; Einstein himself, however, said that the roots of his intellectual development of relativity grew instead from his wonder at what would happen if he ran faster than light. This marvelous conundrum had been a preoccupation of his since the age of sixteen.

In 1869 F. A. Kekulé advanced his theory that the six carbon atoms of benzene were arranged in a hexagon. He claimed that he had seen "a vision of a snake with its tail in its mouth" and that this vivid image made him consider the now familiar arrangement of carbon atoms in aromatic compounds, a possibility that had previously eluded him.

In 1858 Alfred Russel Wallace, who originated the theory of evolution at the same time Charles Darwin did, had what he called his "flash of light while in the middle of a severe intermittent fever at Tanape in the Malay peninsula." Although too fever-shaken to be able to put pen to paper, he "waited anxiously for the termination of my fit" and then wrote off to his friend Darwin.

The great poet, engraver, and visionary William Blake is a classic example of one who felt himself constantly in touch with other worlds and other gods. At a time when he was little known and completely neglected, Blake constantly claimed to be one of the greatest English poets. None of the critical establishment at that time agreed for one moment, and many said he was mad. More than a century after Blake's death, two major poets, W. B. Yeats and A. E. Housman, agreed that Blake's is the purest poetry ever written. We may suppose that what Blake said was true and that his vision of himself, shared by almost no one else, was correct.

Vincent van Gogh is known to have sold only one picture during his lifetime. Much of the last year of his life was spent in a mental hospital suffering from what seems to have been a schizophrenic illness that started in his early twenties. His astounding, wonderful pictures seem to have been a desperate attempt to hold reality in check; even today, reality seems to burst forth from the canvas, as if it could hardly be contained there.

Even the astronauts, who are carefully selected for their practical nature, discuss in mystical terms their going to the moon and beyond—the better to see Earth's lonely splendor in the infinite cosmos and to ponder the great enigma of existence. One even participated in a test of extrasensory perception between Moon and Earth. Is what the astronauts have said less odd than similar views expressed by the mystics? I think not, although it may seem so to many people in the healthy, well-fed, ultrarational Western world, where "strange experiences" are rare and widely disregarded.

Until the last twenty to forty years, people in even the most advanced countries in the world were kept well in touch with the facts of life and death and the strange problems of the cosmos through extraordinary experiences brought about by changes in physiology as a result of disease, starvation in various forms, and other stressful events. Today, the "modern world"—relieved of much of such burdens—seems impaled on the horns of a dilemma. On the one hand is the feeling that the Great Questions will yield to man's rationality—all the while, impressive efforts are being made to affirm that this rationality actually exists. On the other hand, the notion that the possibility of *knowing* the answers to the Great Questions resides in every man—as the transcendentalists maintain—is repugnant to those who have great pride in their rationality and little experience with strange inner occurrences either of their own or of others. The upshot of it all is that the Great Problems are still with us— people still are born and still die, the nature of the cosmos remains a puzzle—and our interest in knowing The Answers remains as great as it has ever been.

Drugs as a Means of Exploring "Transcendentalism"

Because so few people today seem to have what I would call a good understanding of reality, a quite false view of reality is widespread. Many people do not perceive the experiential world as an extraordinary construct of great complexity, great beauty, and great strangeness. They see it all as merely ordinary, which to me is very sad. My feeling is that it would be inexcusably arrogant for us utterly to disregard the thinking on matters of transcendence by some of the greatest human beings who have ever lived. Indeed, I believe that "transcendentalia" should be more thoroughly explored. As it happens, drugs—particularly the hallucinogens or psychedelics—are rather good vehicles for such explorations, and we should not discard them. But we should know their dangers.

Regrettably, a shadow has been cast over much legitimate, careful, and very promising research with psychedelic drugs. Worse, the shadow began to form when it became apparent that these substances—chemicals that, in minute quantities, affect man's most vital organ, his brain—were finding widespread illicit use among the most precious and innocent segments of our population: our children and youth. At the moment, we are faced with a situation in which, in effect, anyone who wants to do so can hop into his own private rocket whenever he feels like it and take off into the unknown without any certain knowledge of either his destination or the possibility that his ship may explode. Inasmuch as the "rockets" we are considering here alter one's perceptions and perspectives, it is remarkable that much more damage has not been done than has been reported. We are not out of danger yet; indeed, the situation is almost certain to become worse.

Behind that pessimistic prediction is the knowledge of man's historic interest in mind-affecting drugs and the enormous difficulty we will have in controlling the use and availability of psychedelics. More of these substances have been discovered (or rediscovered) during the past fifteen years or so than in any other fifteen years in history. It seems likely that more will be found in the immediate future. Some of the new psychedelics will be found in plants; others will be synthesized in chemical laboratories. Each discovery will suggest places in which to look for new and different psychedelics and will point to new—and possibly easier—ways of synthesizing them. Within a quarter-century—probably in a much shorter period—simple processes will be discovered for making reasonably safe psychedelics in any kitchen, basement, or bathroom tub with materials easily available in stores, pharmacies, fields, and gardens.

Some people believe that the best way to avoid these dangers is to cut off all research on psychedelics. This, I fear, would be a grave mistake. It is with knowledge, not ignorance, that we need to face the drug problems ahead. Moreover, psychedelics can play an important role in research in psychiatry, neurology, and psychology. They seem to be of growing therapeutic usefulness in the treatment of chronic alcoholism and in cases of intractable pain from terminal illness. Ceasing research on psychedelics will not prevent clandestine experiments in the synthesis and use of the substances: forbidden fruit not only tastes sweeter, it draws esoteric interest. Quite likely, a sort of underground, "occult" science would develop which would be deplorable and might be very dangerous.

THE EXPERIENCE OF SCHIZOPHRENIA

My own interest in hallucinogenic drugs stemmed from my work on a theory of schizophrenia with Dr. John Smythies in England in 1950 and 1951. I took mescaline myself for the first time then to make sure I agreed with John about the possibility of simulating with drugs the perceptual experience of psychosis, as described by patients and in literary accounts such as Thomas Hennell's *The Witnesses*. The astonishing similarity between psychotic perceptions and the effects of hallucinogenic drugs is evident in the opening passages of this chapter. That experience was, in a sense, a turning point in my professional life. I quickly gave up the view that mentally ill people are reporting symbolic matters; I realized that what they discuss is their *experience*.

Dr. Smythies, Dr. Abe Hoffer, and I took this matter a good deal more seriously than saying merely, "Well, they're telling the truth after all!"

EXPERIMENTAL DRUG TAKING—HUXLEY, LEARY

Others had known for centuries that schizophrenics were telling the truth—"their truth." What my colleagues and I decided to do—which is what I think of as the "revolutionary" aspect to our approach—was to develop a way of *measuring* the objective differences between the worlds of madness and sanity. (This is explained in Chapter 8.) Our decision led to an extensive series of experiments with psychedelic drugs for simulating the world of madness. Unlike many of our colleagues, we did not feel that it was enough merely to know that changes in a person's world can and do occur under the influence of chemicals; we felt it important—vital, even—to *experience* these things ourselves, for the simple reason that accounts of altered experience by people who have never undergone them would hardly be any more convincing than a book on physical love by a eunuch.

It was through our own personal experiences with mescaline that Dr. Smythies and I became aware of the psychological, artistic, philosophical, and religious implications of the use of these substances. One of the unexpected consequences of our first paper on this subject was an encouraging letter from Aldous Huxley, in which he suggested that we visit him in Los Angeles. The opportunity came, strangely enough, in a matter of weeks, when I went to southern California for a psychiatric meeting. I took with me a few capsules of the cactus alkaloid mescaline, for Smythies and I had decided that our efforts in exploring drug-induced changes in one's perceptual world would benefit greatly from cooperation by those most able to describe experience and whose perceptions were already well sharpened by many years of thought and inquiry. Aldous Huxley obviously filled our bill of particulars perfectly. I still look fondly at my picture of him, gazing down on Los Angeles from the hills through mescalinized eyes—an experience that served as a prelude to his writing *The Doors of Perception.*

It is important to emphasize that Aldous, while lending enthusiastic support to exploration of the worlds of psychedelics for a variety of purposes, knew of the potential difficulties and did not promote the use of psychedelics, as latter-day Pied Pipers of the drug culture have done. He was sufficiently interested in the potential of psychedelics and their hazards to intervene for Hoffer, Smythies, and me with the Ford Foundation on our application for funds to conduct research on these substances. We told the Foundation in particular candor that we did not know how much grace we would have before widespread access to these powerful drugs became a reality—perhaps through "bathtub" home labs. Of course, the primary thrust of our request was for studies of the physiological, philosophical, and religious aspects of psychedelic effects. The Foundation's reply to Aldous, when he saw Ford about the matter, was that the work was too daring, too far out, and might even be dangerous for the Foundation. Aldous wrote to me:

I am afraid there is nothing good to report. The mesozoic reptiles of the Ford Foundation are being as mesozoic as ever. Hutchins, whom I saw two weeks ago when my brother Julian, here on his way to Australia, and Hutchins came to dinner, reports that he has received no word from ———, nor any word from the head of the education department to whom, on my recommendation, he had recommended the work of Samuel Renshaw, of [Ohio State University], in the field of training the special senses and the memory. It looks, I am afraid, as though the FF were finished. The Trustees are so frightened of doing anything unconventional—for whenever the Foundation gets any adverse publicity, people go to the nearest Ford dealer and tell him that henceforward they will buy Chevvies—that the one overriding purpose is now to do nothing at all. The ideal programme for the

Foundation will be to give every professor in the country ten thousand dollars, on condition that he goes on doing exactly what he is doing now. . . . My brother Julian, who has been trying to get the FF to back a grandiose scheme for producing some generally acceptable *weltanschauung*, a little more realistic than orthodox physicalism, found everything completely blocked by ———. So the outlook for our research in mescaline doesn't seem to be too good in this quarter. However, Hutchins has recently flown to New York and has promised to do what he can with the saurians. I only hope he may prove successful.

In fact, it seems that *supporting* our research, rather than rejecting it as Ford did, would have been the more prudent move. Had Ford lent support in the early fifties, we might not be in the sort of situation we find ourselves in today with regard to drugs. Our greater knowledge would have given us better controls. Of course, at that time there was no "clear and present danger" from these drugs on a national or global scale. Timothy Leary wasn't then even on the horizon with what later became a kind of "psychedelic children's crusade."

Aldous and I met Timothy in 1960, on the November night of John Kennedy's election to the presidency. (Coincidentally, Aldous and Kennedy were to die on the same day in 1963.) Leary was dressed in a gray flannel suit and had very short-cut hair. His serious countenance and brilliant blue eyes made him appear the typical young American college professor. He had great personal charm, very likably appearing the serious, sensitive, respectable former West Pointer that he was, obviously imaginative and intelligent. We had a good time with him, and he explained to us, with deep sincerity, how scientific his interest in psychedelic studies was. When we left, Aldous told me how fortunate he felt it was that the work was going to be done at Harvard in the very department that had been started by William James. The only thing that worried me at the time was that I thought Timothy was a bit stuffy!

There was no doubt that Timothy was sincerely devoted to Aldous's point of view, as Tim saw it. It seems incredible, however, that the ten years of theatrics that followed could have been interpreted by Timothy as an attempt to follow Aldous's precept "to do good stealthily." There was no necessity, of course, for Leary to subscribe to Aldous's ideas, but the point is that he claimed to be doing so. Judging from my occasional talks with Leary since, I don't believe that he was in the least bit insincere; I'm sure that he wasn't stupid.

Aldous's vision was well organized, with a remarkable capacity for what one might call broad and deep linearity. He spanned past, present, and future and related possibility to probability. In this huge, majestic context, he suggested—with extraordinary gentleness—a course of action that could be attained if good judgment was combined with luck (not omitting, of course, hard and sustained effort, which Aldous never omitted from his calculations). Aldous's prescription was an extremely modest one. It was aimed, above all else, at minimizing the chance of doing harm. As much as anyone I have ever known, he was aware of man's capacity for doing evil by good intentions. He was one of those rare individuals who had taken the measure of himself and his fellows and was seldom self-deluded. There are few who can face the facts of existence consistently, without becoming cynical or carapaced or mad. Aldous remained good-natured, curious, inquiring, kindly and deeply concerned. He did not flinch from what he perceived. His advice was based upon knowledge of himself and his fellows, as well as knowledge of history and psychedelics. It seemed to me then, as it seems now, to have been the best possible advice. But there was one thing that Aldous did not and could not know at that time (1960): how his advice was likely to be perceived by Timothy Leary and just how, in all sincerity, the latter would set about "doing good stealthily."

Aldous's ignorance was not of the usual kind—he did not

neglect this very important aspect of the matter, but he knew very well that we were unable then to explore other people's umwelts. If I had any uneasiness at that time, it was focused in the wrong direction. I feared that the Harvard people would be too rigid, too Skinnerian, too fond of nit-picking. I could have spared myself such worries.

Had Aldous and I had access to the Typology explained in Chapters 2 and 3, we would surely have seen things differently. We would have realized that Timothy only *appeared* to be a sober, calculating, planning, scientific sort, while he was actually a visionary person whose imagination needed constant stimulation and *focus* for him to be able to function in the responsible style of the person he appeared to us to be. As a consequence, Aldous and I made all the wrong moves.

We had been led to expect that Timothy would undertake all planning and development of the research program at Harvard. Timothy is perfectly capable of this sort of thing if his Typology—he is an Extraverted Intuition-Feeling-type—doesn't interfere. What he needed was for us to have made the planning of the research and the experimental design problems as wonderfully interesting and romantic to him as some of the long-range potential consequences of psychedelics seemed to him. As it was, he developed the view that psychedelic substances merely triggered peak experience and, therefore, exactly what they were or how they worked did not really matter—the experience was all.

To Timothy, it didn't really matter if many people fell by the wayside, because the object was to create the greatest benefit for the greatest number. This is a millennialist's view of history, very much the same as the outlook of another Intuition-Feeling-type, Adolf Hitler. I think that if we had appealed to Timothy's imagination on another level, he would not have gone on repeating the same mistake over and over as he did. It's simply not chic to repeat mistakes. Fools say they learn by experience, but I prefer instead, as Bismarck said, "to learn by other people's experience." Surely Timothy could have benefited from some of the experiences already attained in this field.

Timothy, who has taken psychedelics on a great many occasions, is typologically the sort of person who needs this kind of stimulation like he needs a hole in the head. An expansive, expanding, highly imaginative mind like his requires psychedelics infrequently, if ever more than once. In fact, the person who most needs them—one who combines Sensation and Thinking functions in a view of the world that is highly territorial in comparison with the expansive view of the other two functional types—is either least likely to use psychedelics or requires a great deal of care and help in their use because of the constricted nature of his mind. The other side of the paradox, illustrated by Timothy's case, is that the person most likely to enjoy psychedelics will probably get along very well without them. Young people, who can often sense "intimations of immortality" as they "put aside the dirty devices of the world," for these and other reasons probably do not need psychedelics at all. Older people, on the other hand, might do well to consider using psychedelics for an equally great variety of reasons: gaining glimpses into other worlds as they enter middle life and tend to become a trifle stale; encouraging development of latent artistic talents; finding ways of coming to grips with some of the profound philosophical questions of life and death as they approach the end of their lives. Psychedelics have been very useful in cases of terminal illness; Aldous himself made use of this potential.

Hard Drugs (Such as Heroin) and Schizophrenia

Hard drugs such as heroin are almost diametrically different from the psychedelics. A colleague distinguishes between the two by their intrinsic distinctiveness from one another: psychedelics are "heads up," because they are mind-stimulating substances, and drugs in the heroin family are "heads down," because they make one dreamy and quiet. At least partly because of these differences, the two kinds of mind-affecting substances appeal to different people in different ways, although there is some overlap. By contrast, there is very little overlap between drinkers and users of drugs, particularly heroin. In studies of these matters in Princeton, we have run across two groups—an alcohol-using unit and a drug-taking unit. They are very keen not to mix with one another; in fact, the drug takers refer to the others as "dirty drunks," while the alcohol unit calls the drug takers "those drug fiends."

A study of drug abuse in New Jersey by the state Law Enforcement Program Assistance Agency in 1970 revealed that there were perhaps 7,000 narcotics addicts, each with a $30-a-day habit. If that is correct, some rather interesting deductions may be made. Most authorities who are medically or psychiatrically qualified believe that between 15 and 25 percent of all hard-drug users are, in fact, schizophrenics who are trying to treat themselves. Thus, at least 1,000 of New Jersey's 7,000 narcotics addicts are probably schizophrenic, but there are probably far more. It would seem, then, that a substantial part of the state's narcotics addiction problem is really not so much socio-medico-legal-economic as it is medico-psychiatric. Schizophrenia!

From this point of view, in order to provide effective treatment, one would want to know whether a particular individual is suffering from narcotics addiction or from narcotics addiction and schizophrenia. Plain addiction, if it responds, is likely to continue to improve as long as drugs are avoided; schizophrenia in an addict without antipsychotic treatment will probably become worse and worse as drugs are avoided for longer and longer periods.

It seems that our own tests (see Chapter 8), combined with

the quantitative electroencephalogram and certain other objective measures, put us in a position, right now, to exclude schizophrenics from some of the rigorous antinarcotics treatments that are likely to hurt them more than help them. There is no reason to suppose, for instance, that group interaction is likely to benefit those whose narcotics addiction is combined with schizophrenia. To the contrary, we know that group interaction can be harmful to schizophrenics under certain circumstances. Not only would identification of schizophrenia in addicts be of great benefit to them, but in the long run it would save drug-abuse control agencies considerable money.

We believe schizophrenics turn to narcotics sometimes in an effort to treat their illness. Opiates are quite effective in reducing the impact of schizophrenia's symptoms and were even used in the treatment of insanity in the 1850s. The trouble was that a person so treated became constipated, then got hooked on the opiate. At the time, however, narcotics addiction wasn't a bad bargain, for many schizophrenics died from suicide, exhaustion, and their peculiar propensity for tuberculosis and upper respiratory infections (probably resulting from an upset in the schizophrenic's adrenaline and histamine metabolism which interferes with his developing a fibrous response to his pulmonary illness).

Alcohol and Schizophrenia

Many of today's schizophrenics become hooked on either opiates or alcohol. Our studies have shown, in fact, that about one-third of all alcoholics are schizoid, many of them resorting to alcohol as a kind of tranquilizer to lessen the impact of their mental illness. As we have found with schizophrenic drug addicts, it is better to treat schizophrenic alcoholics first as schizophrenics and second as alcoholics.

An admirable schizophrenic alcoholic I knew in Boston told his doctors, who were trying to treat his alcoholism, "If you can find something better than alcohol for preventing the terrible experiences I have, give it to me, and I'll take it." The doctors never found anything better. Tranquilizers made the schizophrenic alcoholic feel very unwell and generally "flattened out" in mood. He stuck to his alcoholic guns until he began to take niacin, and now, several years later, he insists that he is "just beginning to live after thirty years." This man is a very intelligent Thinking-type, who probably suffered considerably from what he himself must have regarded as a lack of principles in his use of alcohol. He has his principles now, however, and is working away very well indeed, making up for all that lost time.

The association between schizophrenia and alcoholism has had some unexpected fringe benefits.

SCHIZOPHRENICS ANONYMOUS

The first Schizophrenics Anonymous chapter was founded in Saskatoon in the mid-1960s by ex-patients of Dr. Abram Hoffer, who felt that they wanted an organization resembling Alcoholics Anonymous, where they could discuss their troubles, give each other support, and encourage schizophrenics who had not yet got to treatment to do so. Since then, the organization has spread slowly but steadily, and is developing groups in both Canada and the United States, particularly on the coasts.

The late Bill W., who co-conceived A.A. and whom Dr. Hoffer and I had known for many years and who became a great personal friend, evinced much interest in the development of Schizophrenics Anonymous. He encouraged, as he had done in the case of A.A., the development of a wise balance of the medical and the religious. The great importance of religion is to sustain hope and faith while medicine pursues its often slow and halting course. Bill W. became particularly interested in the fact that our findings suggested that a substantial proportion of alcoholics—as much as a third in some samples and at least 10 percent in nearly all samples—demonstrated perceptions very similar to those suffering from schizophrenia. His own experience with A.A. fully supported this, and he decided to pass the information along to doctors who he knew were interested in treating alcoholics and alcoholism. Among these doctors were David Hawkins and Russell Smith. Dr. Hawkins has given several thousand schizophrenics and several hundred schizophrenic alcoholics the megavitamin (niacin) treatment; Dr. Smith has treated hundreds of alcoholics, whether schizophrenic or not. Bill W.'s great interest in these matters continued right up to the end of his life. He published two valuable pamphlets which he distributed to A.A. doctors and other interested professionals, and was planning a third at the time of his death in 1971. Schizophrenics, like alcoholics before them, benefit greatly from an organization like S.A., partly at least because the association reinforces the idea that they have a severe illness about which they must learn if they are to be responsible patients rather than mere victims of misfortune.

TYPOLOGY: THE SCHIZOPHRENIC ALCOHOLIC

What makes certain schizophrenics, and not others, turn to alcohol? Having seen a good many of these cases, but not having done a proper study of them as yet in the way I would wish, I can say that I have a definite clinical *impression*—by no means concrete evidence—that alcoholism tends to affect most strongly either schizophrenics who combine Sensation and Thinking functions or schizophrenics whose Typology conflicts strongly with demands made upon them. In these cases, alcohol is used as a cushion against misfortune. That is, schizophrenics who turn to alcohol for relief tend either to be combinations of Thinking and Sensation functions or combinations of the other two types trying to function in the mode of the Sensation and Thinking "commonsense world." Similarly, psychedelic drugs would be hardest on the *normal* Sensation and Thinking combination because the drug-modified world also runs counter to the ST's or TS's native common sense.

Niacin: Help for Schizophrenics, Psychedelic Drug Users, Alcoholics

As was seen in Chapter 5, niacin seems to reduce the disorder of the schizophrenic's world. It does the same with the distorted world of the psychedelic drug user, perhaps by a similar mechanism. The only snag with taking the large amounts of niacin needed to reduce the effects of psychedelic drugs—to "bring down" a person from a "bad trip"—is that it produces a large flush and itching for a short while. This can be quite alarming, if unexpected, and very annoying, whether you expect it or not. It is infinitely preferable to the bad trip, however. Actually, one can avoid the flush altogether, although a headache may be suffered in the bargain, if instead of niacin, or nicotinic acid (vitamin B_3), one takes the amide, niacinamide, or nicotinamide, which can also damp a psychedelic high. Both compounds seem to work as well at this as tranquilizers and do not have the collateral "flattening" effects that tranquilizers produce.

Some law-enforcement officers in Chicago, in fact, take people who suffer bad trips to a psychiatrist who "brings them down" with niacin. The police are grateful for this, because they are confronted with thousands of young people who are using these drugs—often under the worst possible circumstances—and are "tripping out" in ways that endanger themselves and others. Punitive reactions to the problem have lost their appeal to the police, who have found a way—the niacin-administering psychiatrist—of temporizing until more effective controls are found and instituted.

I should add that niacin has been used with great effect in the treatment of alcoholism, whether schizophrenic or not. Perhaps the most striking effects of the niacin treatment of alcoholism have been reported by Dr. Russell Smith. According to an early study of his, in which 507 hard-core alcoholics were treated with massive doses of niacin and given psychotherapeutic support, 371 had achieved sobriety; all had been treatment failures prior to Dr. Smith's work. This represents a recovery rate of 73 *percent* over a period of two years, nearly all of them subsequently maintained in Alcoholics Anonymous.

Following that success, Dr. Smith was given a large grant by the local highway-control officials. The grant was said to have been based upon a great and as yet not completely understood drop in traffic deaths in his area. It appeared that some highway people ascribed this to Dr. Smith's efforts more positively even than he did himself. How could Dr. Smith's work have accounted for a drop in highway deaths (if, indeed, it did)?

I had always supposed that the social drinker was the main source of fatal accidents, but the evidence does not support that view. The drinkers most often found to be at fault are not by any stretch of the imagination "social drinkers" but the real "pros," chronic alcoholics; amateur drinkers would be anesthetized at blood levels of 0.15 or 0.20 percent. It appears that a sudden change for the better in several hundred chronic alcoholics who were restricted to a fairly small area might, indeed, have the effect Dr. Smith described from his work around Ann Arbor.

If the highway people are correct, it would seem that we are in a position to make a major change in the highway fatality rate by concentrating on a rather small section of the population: genuinely ill alcoholics. It should be relatively easy to pick up alcoholics early and encourage them to get adequate treatment. This could be done systematically in matters like automotive driving, which is regulated by law. There can be little doubt that anything that would prevent this slaughter of alcoholics and their thousands of victims would be very desirable—and should have a high priority.

In addition, this is the kind of approach that is likely, once understood, to get support from the public, police, and judges. All the evidence at present suggests that it is not the public unwillingness for new approaches that is at fault, but the disinclination of the professions (psychiatry and psychology in particular) to depart from their traditions and produce approaches that are promising and feasible. Producing treatments that can be applied to only a few people—however excellent their results—is not particularly helpful. The most cogent criticism of most treatments suggested in the last quarter-century for the big psychiatric illnesses has been: Even if they work, can they be used for the benefit of hundreds of thousands of patients? The answer has nearly always been "No!"

The Future of Today's Drug Culture

What is the future of today's drug culture? Of psychedelic drugs? Clearly, the psychedelics should not be looked upon as the absolute instrument for entering new and useful worlds of experience. This is, after all, a potential of mind. Psychedelics do give us a way of studying this potential, however, and they seem to be better than most available techniques for exploring worlds of altered states of consciousness. Various forms of yoga and meditation are being used for these purposes today. While they may be good, they certainly do not produce the sort of experience in most people that psychedelics do so impressively and, in many cases, so usefully.

Grave dangers exist in the widespread use of psychedelic drugs such as LSD and mescaline. While I seriously doubt that the evidence of chromosomal damage from LSD is convincing —and many share my doubts who are better qualified than I to have an opinion on the matter—there are other dangers which are known and must be guarded against, as well as some yet to be discovered.

We know that these drugs may trigger psychotic episodes in schizophrenics and may send quite normal people on harrowing "bad trips" under the right (or "wrong") circumstances. Finding methods of preventing tragedies from psychedelics will call for greater governmental understanding of the problem. This can be achieved only through further research and a more enlightened attitude toward the drug problem than is evidenced by most authorities today. I believe it is not too much to say that finding and instituting ways of protecting people from hazards that are measurable and controllable—as those from drugs unquestionably are—is government's *responsibility*, and one which an informed public can help government accept.

Prudery: Sexual and Psychopharmacological

During a visit to Columbus, Ohio, where I spoke to physicians and educators regarding psychedelics, I was impressed by the real agitation and anxiety bordering on panic that these amiable people showed. It struck me that somewhere or other I had come across those desperate questions before: "How can we know when they are taking drugs?" "What shall we do about it?" "Will they confide in us?" Et cetera. The shadow of ruined young lives dominated the meetings and cast some gloom over the whole affair. Moral exhortations were made from time to time with appeals for "strengthening family ties," "improving community relations," "more spiritual values," etc. Then I recalled some of those tremendous Victorian treatises on masturbation's causing madness. The doom-ridden atmosphere had the authentic flavor of those grand days when anxietymaking was one of the main occupations of moral folk. I wonder whether things have changed. May not the medical historian of twenty or thirty years hence, or possibly even less, find our overconcern just as odd, irrational, and absurd as we now find those grand Victorian prophets of doom with their specially designed anti-masturbatory devices which were available in London only thirty years or so ago?

It suddenly struck me: While we have become more outspoken in sexual matters during the twentieth century, we have become much prissier and much more censorious about drugs.

Take Sherlock Holmes. Who will forget Watson's concern over the master detective's devotion to his work, the long nights spent smoking the strong black shag which he enjoyed so much while he accompanied himself on the violin and from time to time gave himself an injection of that newly discovered drug, cocaine? Thus would Holmes turn his full attention to a case. Watson was concerned, of course, because his friend did not get a good night's rest, but the black shag, if I recollect the story properly, gave him as much concern as the cocaine, which had only recently been given the warmest possible commendation by Dr. S. Freud, of Vienna, a young neuroanatomist. The prestige of Viennese medicine was very high indeed at that time, and such information was taken seriously.

However, while Watson is extremely frank about the great detective's drug life, Holmes's love life receives the most cursory attention. It would have been offensive to Victorian taste to have the great detective embroiled with numerous dolls and doxies. *Strand,* the family magazine for which Doyle wrote, would have found it deeply shocking to see Holmes in the embraces of even lightly clothed young ladies (the stories were well illustrated). They were not at all shocked by his violin playing, shag smoking, and cocaine shooting.

Today the situation would be somewhat different. I am sure that many of today's women's magazines would not object to a detective hero who spent much time with more or less unclothed and beautiful ladies. Such illustrations would be considered elevating and educational, ensuring that youngsters who riffled the pages of that particular family magazine were acquainted with the "facts of life," if indeed they needed to be introduced to them. However, a handsome picture of the great detective mainlining cocaine to solve such cases as "The Speckled Band" would be considered not merely risqué but dangerous. I think we could predict that there would be storms of protest. In addition, the idea that a man with whom the highest secrets of state frequently reposed was "drug-dependent," to use a current euphemism for our old friend, "dope fiend," would seem wholly implausible.

Memories of Aldous Huxley, the "Gentle Triphibian"

I first met Aldous at his home in Los Angeles in 1953. He glided toward me from the cool darkness of the house into the sunshine of the front porch. He seemed to be suspended just a fraction of an inch above the ground, like one of Blake's allegorical figures. He was very tall. His head was massive, finely shaped, with a splendid brow. The gaze, from his better eye, was keen and piercing, but seemed to be focused a little above and beyond me. His handshake was cool and uncertain, as if he did not enjoy the custom, and this was indeed so, for thin-skinned, lightly built, slender people, whom the somatotypologist William Sheldon calls "cerebrotonic," do not relish physical contact overmuch. His voice was clear and beautifully modulated, with a penetrating, almost birdlike quality.

What impressed me from the start and continued to impress me through the years of our friendship was the kindness and tolerance of this man, whose writings had sometimes led me to suppose that he would be disillusioned, cynical, and even savage.

I had expected Aldous to be well informed, but from our first meeting to our final one in Stockholm in 1963, I never ceased to be delighted by the range, boldness, flexibility, and sheer playfulness of his splendid mind. When he was at ease, he would toss ideas about with the grace, elegance, and sense of fun that a dolphin shows in playing with a ball. It did not matter whether we were attending a scientific meeting, sightseeing in New York, visiting Forest Lawn (the great Los Angeles burying ground), walking on the Surrey Commons (which he loved greatly), bowling across the Mojave Desert, threading our way toward the Athenaeum (where he said, "You can hardly hear yourself think for the whine of political, academic, and ecclesiastical axes being ground"), or making a shopping expedition to Ohrbach's, Aldous would be discussing both serious and trivial matters with his immense fund of expert knowledge. He loved a good gossip: about the latest scientific discovery, theological principles, books, paintings, new developments in sewage treatment, utopias, the water-supply system of Los Angeles—a particular favorite of his—the effect of mass-produced clothing on social and political systems, parapsychology, or the future of megalopolis. The subject of the gossip was less important to him than the occasion it provided him to reflect upon the infinite strangeness of life. Although he was very well informed, he was always learning more, and the best tribute one could get was his delighted, "How absolutely incredible!"

He was proud that he could earn his living by his pen, an

occupation that he enjoyed and for which he had a craftsman's love and concern. He looked upon himself as a writer who should be able to communicate with all kinds of people—not only the learned and the erudite. Consequently, he did not feel it beneath him to write for the films or popular magazines. At one time he was planning to turn *Brave New World* into a musical because he thought its ideas would get across better that way. He wrote for *Playboy* and *Daedalus*, for *Life* and *Encounter*, and considered they were equally acceptable ways of communicating with people.

In spite of remarks that I sometimes heard about "mystical trends" in his later years, I always found him shrewd, matter-of-fact, and to the point. But the history of mysticism—in spite of popular notions to the contrary—has always concerned the practical, hard-headed, socially effective people.

Aldous had got a Dictaphone for the occasion of taking mescaline. I could see no decent way out, and so we agreed to do the experiment. I had a restless night. Next morning, as I stirred the water and watched the silvery white mescaline crystals swirling down and dissolving with a slightly oily slick, I wondered whether it would be enough or too much. Aldous and Maria (his first wife) would be sad if it did not work. But what if it worked *too* well? Should I cut the dose in half? The setting could hardly have been better. It was a delicious May morning in Hollywood, no hint of smog to make the eyes smart, not too hot. Moreover, Aldous seemed an ideal subject, Maria eminently sensible, and we had all taken to each other, which was very important for a good experience. But I did not relish the possibility—however remote—of being "the man who drove Aldous Huxley mad." My fears were groundless. The bitter chemical did not work as quickly as Aldous had expected, for he was a bit impatient. It slowly etched away the patina of conceptual thinking, and the doors of perception were cleansed. Aldous began to see things less impeded by his enormous rationalizing brain. Within two and a half hours, I knew that it was acting, and after three hours I was sure that all would go well, and it did. Aldous and Maria were greatly pleased, and so was I. In addition, I was much relieved.

I had enjoyed myself and looked forward to Aldous's report, which has become widely known as *The Doors of Perception*. From then on, we usually saw each other at least once a year and were always writing. His last letter was written on October 15, 1963. He was discussing the outline of a study of human potential upon which we were jointly engaged. It is characteristic of him: "But being like the old man of Thermopylae, who never does anything properly, I can't lay my hands on the carbon of it." The letter ends, "I feel I shall never again be good for anything, but I hope and think this state of affairs will pass in due course ('it will pass'—the only motto good for every human situation, good or bad)."

It was when he was writing *Island* that I learned about the cancer that was to kill him. In November 1960, the day of the presidential election, I had flown to see him in Cambridge, Massachusetts, where he was lecturing. He looked worn, tired, and pale. He told me that he had a cancer of the tongue but that his doctor thought it had a good chance of responding to X-ray treatment. He had considered surgery but, learning that it would almost certainly interfere with his speech, had decided against it. He asked me not to discuss this with Laura (his second wife, after Maria's death) or other members of his family, because they would worry, and it would not help him. He then dismissed the matter and read me the chapter from *Island* dealing with the Moksha medicine, the use of psychedelics for helping people prepare themselves to change for the better and how to prepare themselves for dying. It is, I believe, packed with his finest ideas, which will repay much study and consideration. It has still to be fully appreciated.

Early in 1961 he and Laura lost their new house in a furious brush fire, and all Aldous's possessions, including his books and papers, were burned. It was a sort of death, a stripping away of everything; as he said later, "I took it as a sign that the grim reaper was having a good look at me." Yet he weathered this, too, and on his visits to England in 1961 and 1962, although thin—you felt a gust of wind would blow him away—he was wonderfully lively.

In his last August in Stockholm, at the World Academy, he was transparently pale and had been unsure whether he could come at all. The cancer had returned, but had been beaten back again, for the time being. Yet he worked zealously to persuade members of the Academy to study human potential. Having succeeded, he set to and prepared an outline. I sat with him while he was completing this in his hotel room. He was engrossed in his work, and watching him I felt that I might never see him again. He told me that it was no easier to write now than it had been twenty-five years before. He knew of no shortcuts to good writing, only repeated rewriting.

I was uneasy when we parted, but tried to ignore my misgivings. He was to visit me in Princeton during October, only two months away. And in our last few minutes together, we were discussing who should be invited to participate in the new work. But when October came, he was too ill to travel. The borrowed time gained by X-ray treatment had run out, and soon my dear friend, the wise and gentle triphibian, for "triphibian" was his own definition of man, was no more.

7
The Special Worlds of Violence

The Universality of Violence

We all have the capacity to behave violently and the tendency, under certain circumstances, to fulfill that capacity with acts of violence. This has been demonstrated convincingly and repeatedly throughout history with awful effectiveness by even the most pacific peoples, many of whom have professed nonviolence as part of their way of life. The Hindu-Muslim wars are a good example.

The fact that all humans are able to behave violently if the appropriate chord is struck does not mean that man is necessarily a violent creature by nature, as some "authorities" on behavior have been arguing recently. While man does not need to have a gene for violence in his evolutionary heritage, it would be inconceivable for us to have come as far as we have without at least a complement of genes which, in certain combinations, would enable us to act violently in situations in which violent action was necessary for survival.

Violence, then, is universal within the species, but attitudes toward violence and capacities for acting violently are highly particularized matters. This is true on the level of the individual and on the level of the coherent group as well, whether it is a social, religious, or political organization, a nation, or an entire culture. Viewed in historical perspective, many of our recent experiences with violence—from assassination and multiple murder to riot, revolution, and war—can instruct us in the nature of violent human behavior so that we may understand it better, predict it, and even prevent its occurrence, or at least lessen the severity of its consequences. Such understanding can have effects at all levels of human transaction, from global to personal. The key, again, is in understanding other people's worlds.

MAO TSE-TUNG AND THE CHINESE

Much concern has been expressed in the West in recent years over the contribution Mao Tse-tung and the Chinese might make toward international instabilities which could lead to the violence of nuclear war. It is extremely important, first of all, to realize that Chairman Mao's world is very different from ours. Mao is one of the great megatypes, a powerful Extraverted Feeling-Intuitive-type. But, above all, he is a *Chinese* Feeling-Intuitive, with the Chinese capacity for xenophobia and the great Chinese pride. In addition, Mao is a poet, self-proclaimed fountainhead of all true communism, and a great warrior who has experienced and understands extremely violent actions very well. It has long been his vision to reshape his country completely. Although he is a remarkably sensitive man who wrote a poem to the husband of a dead friend, he accepted the inevitability of breaking quite a few of the 750 million Chinese "eggs" to create the ideal communist omelet. Considering only this can be very unsettling if one does not keep in mind the fact that Mao is operating always from a Chinese context. One must consider, also, what the Chinese attitudes are toward war. No one has been more interested in this matter than Bernard Law Montgomery, a great admirer and personal friend of Mao's

(Montgomery is discussed in Chapter 3). The Englishman has pointed out that throughout their history the Chinese have never taken the military arts very seriously, and he doubts that they ever will in the long haul—because they have never generally held the warrior in high esteem. Indeed, Montgomery doesn't believe that Mao himself thinks much of the warrior.

At the root of these conclusions is Monty's awareness that Mao doesn't really *believe* in technical war. His idea of war is entirely different from the concept of a contest involving a "citizen army" and all that. His idea is: *all the people in a total struggle*—ultimately to liberate the human (Chinese) spirit from artificial constraints. From this, it should be perfectly clear that the world has little to worry about from Mao or his people insofar as their instigating a global war is concerned; "all the people" in the "total struggle" are not at war against other peoples and are not going to go one foot beyond their borders, especially if the people do not take the military arts seriously. I think the Chinese are signaling to us very effectively that although they wish to spread Chinese influence as far as they can, they simply do not intend to venture far outside their national borders. It is all the more difficult to look upon the Chinese today as an invasive and aggressive power because, for the past two thousand years, they have been among the *least* invasive and aggressive people in the world. We should take this very seriously. We should *not* make the Chinese feel that we hold them in contempt, but we should make it clear that we respect their intrinsically nonaggressive nature and keep this in mind in our interpretations of their actions.

HITLER AND THE GERMANS

We have a quite different situation in the case of Hitler and the Germans. Hitler was also a megatype—an Extraverted Intuitive-Feeling-type—but one who perhaps was psychotic at times. His expansive, visionary temperament and mental illness (assuming he had one) seem to have run parallel courses. And he enjoyed the great good luck—for him, at least—of having the Germans, through folly and miscalculation, provide him with a very special form of occupational therapy on a grand scale. The fact that Hitler was probably severely mentally disturbed at times did not prevent him from being extraordinarily acute, highly intelligent, and astoundingly inspiring. The Germans, being a calculating people, calculated how to make use of Corporal Hitler. To do so safely and effectively, however, they would have to take the measure of the man. As a German leader said later, Hitler was a "man without measurement"—a marvelously shrewd remark, for Hitler was completely boundless in his way, despite the vulgarity of his detestable visions. It was too late when the German people sensibly decided to rid themselves of the corporal. You don't put an inspiring man with rich and pathological feelings in the saddle and get him out again very easily. In running a war for methodical, commonsense people who take military arts seriously, Hitler was a really terrible menace because he lacked almost all of the ordinary restraints of a well human being. His inspired visions came to have fewer and fewer relationships to the actual facts.

One might ask, then, how it was possible for Hitler to achieve group consensus on many of the Nazi party actions. Actually, many Nazi activities were results of group decisions only to the extent that some of the worst acts were not undertaken by Hitler individually. The murder of mental patients in Germany, for example, was not initiated by Hitler and was not approved by Hitler; those murders were actually stopped by him. Human experimentation was undertaken not by the Nazis or the military, but by German medical scientists apparently without any stimulus from Hitler at all. Nevertheless, these crimes rightfully belonged to the Führer, whose crucial contribution to them was his creation of a climate in which diabolic activity became the accepted style.

The "Visionary-Violence" Syndrome—Hitler, Oswald, Manson

Generally speaking, people who rejoice in violence in most societies are, most of the time, those who see violence as an *opportunity* for some great visionary developments which most other people do not want to happen or, at best, about whose feasibility they are very dubious. Once violence begins to get under way, however, it is a whole new ball game. The "ordinary" people become puzzled, uncertain, and worried. Their uneasiness does not reduce the probability of their becoming involved in "extraordinary" affairs—perhaps even those involving violence—because the people become more likely to listen to extreme ideas under extraordinary conditions. These circumstances provide fertile soil for escalation of irrationality until individuals start popping up with ideas that—viewed away from the induced irrational context—appear to be utterly insane; for example, the conviction that total disintegration of society cannot but be all to the good. That, in fact, was the cry during several of the college campus riots in the late sixties.

Those riots illustrate another queer aspect to the "visionary-violence syndrome": after it is all over, the instigators are terribly hard to find. They seem to disappear into the woodwork and generally are hard to remember. They seem to stand out only in a context in which other people are exceptionally dismayed over the action, and only very rarely does that context persist for any length of time (consider again the campus riots). Hitler and the Nazis constituted a notable exception. The magic of Hitler remains an almost impenetrable mystery to this day, even to men like Albert Speer who were immersed in it. I do not believe Speer's confusion and puzzlement over that violent episode is either guilt or denial. He seems to be a very honest man trying to analyze an experience of a kind that is not susceptible to the analysis of one who appears, as Speer does, to be an Extraverted Thinking-Sensation-type and a highly intelligent one. Speer got himself mixed up with an immensely diabolical individual and learned only that the devil is not a figure to be tampered with.

Two other violent visionaries whose exploits become comprehensible only through an understanding of their own worlds are President Kennedy's assassin, Lee Harvey Oswald, and Charles Manson, the hippie guru whose "family" of sick young girls and one utter madman committed the multiple murders in California in 1969. Manson, like Hitler, was an Extraverted Intuition-Feeling-type. Oswald, an Intuition-Thinking-type, was devoted to grand themes, a true millennialist who, according to his diary, wanted not merely to precipitate a local misfortune in the death of the president of the United States but to trigger World War III, out of which he would emerge (how, he never made clear) to be "remembered for 10,000 years" as the initiator of a "new era." (I wonder whether it occurred to him that no human has been remembered that long.)

Manson's intuition served another purpose: it inspired others to follow him toward goals that were often absurd or even obscene. His special charm for girls made him look all the more like a mini-Hitler. The Führer also had a remarkable effect upon women, but Manson either could not or did not manage to extend this charm to men, as Hitler did with great effect (although, as Speer points out, Hitler was much more comfortable in the company of women than of men). If Hitler and Manson were, indeed, Intuition-Feeling-types, they would also share the ambiguity of possessing two leading functions whose qualities are usually associated with femininity while at the same time demonstrating the male preoccupation with groups (as anthropologist Lionel Tiger has described).

Manson's murderousness, like Hitler's, seems to be closely connected with his typological qualities and is wholly different from that of someone like Stalin, who was too unimaginative to see any way out of his political difficulties other than mass terror. Possession of imagination does not, of course, make murderousness any less heinous, but it does make it qualitatively different. Manson believed that group solidarity (morality) was enhanced by shared feeling-experiences; sex, living together, and murdering together were, it seems, aimed at achieving this. Those who defected and denied his charisma were considered disloyal and were made to suffer to enhance the group loyalty. There is no evidence at all that Stalin considered it important to enhance loyalty or inspire people. He manipulated people, and since terror was an available means of manipulation in Russia at the time, Stalin used terror.

Manson's scheme was not unlike Hitler's in its objective: to precipitate a holocaust—involving Negroes, as Hitler had used the Jews—which would create a situation that would be beneficial to him and expand his authority and influence. Manson's capacity for planning seems to have been very slight, and his whole plan was carried out on a minute—or at least highly localized—scale. Manson at least had a scheme, skimpy as it was, which was more than Hitler seems to have had back in 1921, or even in 1927, when all the best authorities of the day were convinced that success was utterly impossible for him. Hitler needed a miracle, according to those prognostications; it seems that a miracle, by the grace of the devil, was exactly what he got.

Manson, Oswald, and Hitler had one other characteristic in common; they all seem to have suffered mental illness. Oswald was diagnosed as schizoid as a youngster, though we do not know how accurate that diagnosis was. His later behavior shows little to conflict with that interpretation, however. Manson's mother said, "Charlie's always been crazy." It would seem almost that being mad is a prerequisite for really grandiose violence, and I suspect there is more than a grain of truth in this. Violence certainly does occur as a result of sane, small-scale crime, of course. You don't have to be mad to supplement a simple robbery with violence; you may think you'll get away with it, but there can be an accident that results in violence—and possibly rather extensive violence involving several people. Not all robbers are efficient. At the same time, the ordinary professional criminal—and even the rank amateur—is no damned fool; all he is after is the cash or something else that makes ordinary sense. Going for the really grand sort of thing —like World War III—takes something special, like a little madness.

Cornered (Defensive) Violence

The sort of violence in which those men indulged can be classified as offensive behavior (to put it mildly). There is violent behavior that is defensive, too, and this form seems to be a great deal more prevalent than one might suspect. In fact, a very large proportion of all violent behavior, however ill-directed, is perceived by its perpetrators as being self-defensive.

We know that there are circumstances in which animals are threatened when even the most timid will fight or attempt to fight. Dr. H. Hediger, director of the Zurich Zoological Parks, showed that the big cats' usual response to someone's approach is retreat, but if you get inside their "attack distance," they advance. Lion and tiger trainers are thus able to maneuver their more or less untamed charges. A cornered rabbit—especially a mother with young—will sometimes fight off and injure a weasel. It is wise not to back even a timid animal into a corner and, if it is in a corner, not to intrude upon its space, for the odds are that it will attack and fight desperately. Skilled policemen and FBI men are very knowledgeable about these matters, and, indeed, they have to be. More than 2,500 years ago, a great Chinese general, Sun Tzu, advised, "Always provide a golden bridge for a fleeing enemy."

A cornered animal or human feels that its social, bodily, and psychological integrity is being threatened and overwhelmed. In such circumstances, violence as a means of self-preservation is both predictable and avoidable. Such invasion of its being may occur because the body boundaries of the self or of others seem fragile or ill-defined. It may occur because others seem bigger or the self seems smaller. Small people are often aggressive, and understandably so.

Predatory Violence

Predators, however, take a different point of view. They perceive certain other creatures as their appointed victims. It seems likely that a person whose perceptions of others become distorted enough for him to see them as animals, subhumans, things, automata, robots, shadows, or merely inferior humans who don't really "count" would have little hesitation in hurting and exploiting these creatures, for such is the underlying nature of offensive violent behavior. This sort of behavior frequently has been expressed when one culture encounters another—the "white man" (pink man) and the American Indian, for example —and it continues to this day (Vietnam and Korea are two stages for this kind of drama). The predator has no qualms about attacking his prey—why should he? That is what it is there for, is it not? I suspect that much of the indifference and lack of remorse shown by at least some "psychopathic" killers can be accounted for by their distorted worlds. Indeed, we have evidence for this, as we shall see later.

Violence from Misperceptions

In addition to the cornered (defensive) and the predatory (offensive), there is a kind of violence arising from misperceptions of status. In most animal societies, dominance and pecking orders are enforced by display and sometimes by combat. Self-perception and changes in one's perceptions of others can easily result in one's inferring changes in status relationships which have not in fact occurred. This may lead to many difficulties, some of which may be resolved by violence.

A MASS KILLER

A tragic example of defensive violence gone wild involves a Saskatchewan farm boy named Victor Hoffman, who felt he was being persecuted by a devil that was seven feet tall and looked like an enormous, bloated black pig. Sometimes it would appear out of the clouds and command him to kill various people and undertake other antisocial acts. Fortunately for young Hoffman, he also had an angel, who gave him support against the pig-devil's onslaught. All of this was deeply disturbing to him, and, being a good and dutiful boy, he went off to a mental hospital to seek help. There, a doctor who was told about the boy's angel assured him that his angel was merely an illusion; somehow, it seems, the conversation between patient and doctor did not penetrate into the matter of the devil. In any case, the good and dutiful boy left the hospital—minus his angel but still bedeviled, to his great distress. He resolved then to see what he could do to his devil that would discourage its attention.

He started by shooting shells at the clouds, but the devil was impervious to these. Eventually, young Hoffman came to the conclusion that his devil was working through some human agency, which he thereupon went out—terrified and armed with his gun—to seek, find, and destroy.

You can imagine him driving through the Saskatchewan parkland, past many little farmhouses with television antennas on top. And suddenly he "knew." As so often happens with mentally ill people, something very familiar is seen and clicks into a new perspective. The antennaed farmhouse he was passing when his "click" occurred was seen by Hoffman, unmistakably, as the devil's headquarters.

He stopped and went up with his gun, determined to shoot the devil's agent. This turned out, unfortunately, to be Farmer Peterson, who was getting up to be about his morning work. The shot that killed him awakened poor Mrs. Peterson and their seven children. By the time Hoffman was through, eight Petersons were dead. Only a little girl was spared, escaping his notice.

Hoffman left, knowing that the devil would put the authorities on to him. He fired out his gun with sand to break up the rifling and make identification of the weapon impossible—at the same time creating evidence for apparent premeditation of the crime.

It didn't take the police long. With their usual rather good sense, they knew that the Petersons were virtuous and good people and that there were no real vendettas in the area. They concluded that the murders could have been done only by someone who was gravely mentally ill. They simply toted up the list of people who had been to mental hospitals and who owned guns. They went right to young Hoffman.

The question was: Was he a murderous boy or wasn't he? According to our tests of him he was very ill and remains so, being shuttled back and forth between hospital and jail in one of those really disgraceful medicolegal muddles.

It is sad to think that Hoffman could have been diagnosed as a schizophrenic in his teens, and kept in the hospital long enough to be treated effectively and thereby purged not just of his angel but of his offending devil too. Today, even the most successful treatment can never remove the appalling memory of that tragedy for him. As in the case of many unlucky schizophrenics, Hoffman had an illness that was not sufficiently noticed until a catastrophe occurred. The only notable distinction about young Hoffman's catastrophe is that it was a big one and could not be swept under the carpet.

It is even sadder to think that Hoffman almost certainly was not concealing anything. He sees himself today and months back as a despairing killer, unable to control himself or his impulses, trapped in a hostile world. It is not quite enough to give a patient electroshock therapy and tranquilizers and tell him, "It's in your imagination." This, in fact, encourages him to see life as the nightmare it has become for him and to act as if it is no more than a nightmare. He is thus helped to avoid action that might allow him to wake up. Hoffman probably did not require much help to avoid such action because, in spite of years of illness, he had never acted before. I would guess that the tranquilizers and electroshock therapy may have served to disinhibit him somewhat. The action he took to break out of his nightmare served also to wipe out all but one of the Peterson family.

I do not suggest that adequate public education about schizophrenia would immediately eliminate all such horrors as this, but it would apply a powerful moral force which is internalized in the great majority of people. People can and should be enjoined that they have no *moral right* to act upon visions, revelations, and notions, however these may have been acquired, without seeking advice from what the Quakers called "certain weighty friends." This may sound fanciful, but the medieval church dealt with visions and visionaries in this way for centuries.

In order to meet such a demand for advice from sick but moral people (who are, by far, the majority of the mentally ill), it is, of course, essential to have adequate instruments available that go beyond the clinical interview. Luckily, we already have at least two of these at hand. (See Chapter 8.) The fact that they exist and that moral people would be expected to check whether they are ill or not would slow down much violence, while at the same time raising steady and sustained doubts about violent solutions generally. The local response to the slaughter in Santa Cruz was to buy more guns and so worsen the general level of safety.

RIOTS AND THE POLICE—HOW TO FEED A POLICEMAN

Handling riots outside of prisons imposes equally strenuous but somewhat different constraints on those trying to quench violence. When a riot begins to escalate, law-enforcement officers are usually hauled in from other jobs or not allowed to go off duty. While this is understandable and necessary, it has certain undesirable consequences. Tired men, and often tense ones, are forced into tension-generating situations. What is more, they probably don't get very well fed. If they are normal North Americans (and which of us would dare say that our police and guardsmen are not?), they will do their best to get a snack, and the odds are that it will be coffee, a Coke, a doughnut, a cookie, or a bar of chocolate. This snack will probably be taken again at intervals. It is about as bad a concoction for coping with a worrying and dangerous situation as one could invent, at least for some people. It may be less dangerous than alcohol, though even this is not by any means certain. In a proportion of these already anxious men, blood sugars will rise steeply and then fall equally quickly; they will feel even more anxious, edgy, and jittery. Among them, trigger-happiness is expectable, even if not excusable. Some men may develop perceptual anomalies, too. Of course, the rioters will doubtless be doing much the same things, but they can go home or to someone else's home when they want to. They are usually unarmed, and are not required to show tact, forbearance, and judgment.

It would seem that we should provide a much more appropriate diet for the police. It should clearly be high in protein and possibly in fat, and low in carbohydrate; ideally, it should probably also contain some antitension (though not tranquilizing) substances. Luckily, we have ascorbic acid available for this. A palatable drink of protein and unsaturated fat, low in carbohydrate, high in ascorbic acid and possibly niacinamide, would be most likely to keep the lawmen relaxed and able to cope. This could be provided to them free; authorities should be encouraged to hand it out among the rioters or would-be rioters, as well. Such a freehanded attitude would not only reduce the chances of a riot, but the drink itself would reduce tension and facilitate accommodations that would help resolve the underlying conflict.

This approach is social, psychological, and physiological. It is also feasible. The drink might be the contribution of a beverage company, which would improve its corporate image while doing market research for a drink that could become extremely popular.

It may seem visionary and improbable, but we have growing evidence to support that this could be the right track to take. While there are many instances of bad food or drink having a disruptive effect on human affairs, there are far fewer of the use of food or drink to prevent a difficult situation from becoming worse. One instance involving a vitamin (C, as we know) enabled Lord Nelson to keep his fleet at sea during a crucial period of the Napoleonic Wars. This great innovation has been said to be as important historically as radar. Napoleon's ships could not stay at sea as long as Nelson's because they did not use oranges and lemons as antiscorbutics.

Institutionalized Mass Violence: War

THE SOCIAL UTILITY OF WAR

At the other end of the spectrum from the individual violence that is born of the despair and dismay of mental illness is a form of mass violence that has been sanctioned and institutionalized by all humanity throughout recorded history—the violence of war. It may seem paradoxical that this form of violence—which is widely equated by statesmen today with madness—usually excludes mentally disturbed people from participation in it because they are a nuisance. It is a gross misconception—and a dangerous one—to call war "madness." War may be ugly, cruel, foolish, menacing, and even hell, in these days of nuclear weapons and fifteen-minute intercontinental delivery systems. But war is decidedly *not* madness. For one thing, the social machinations of warfare alone are much too complicated to be managed by madmen; Hitler demonstrated this very well. For another thing, war has traditionally served the useful purpose of "solving" certain social problems. If we go on thinking of war as madness, we shall be on the wrong track for finding a substitute for this activity whose menace has now far outstripped its social utility. We surely must find a substitute.

Another widespread misconception about war, which has arisen in recent years, is that young men possess an inherent hatred of it. Quite the contrary can be discerned from the poetry of Rupert Brooke. War's almost irresistible appeal to poets is rooted in the romantic visions that warfare evokes in them. It would be only fair for poets to accept a good share of the responsibility for man's warring exploits. Poets have undoubtedly been inspired by war and, in turn, have inspired others, sometimes blowing up small scraps into great sagas. Imagine what effect the *Iliad* must have had. Whatever the Trojan War actually was, it almost certainly was not what Homer wrote about, but more probably just the pursuit of an errant queen or an attempt to attain some commercial trade advantages. Homer, however, wrote about "the topless towers of Ilium" being toppled, and not by human agency, either, but by the gods themselves, in noble battle. One has to be pretty spineless not to wish to do something like that oneself. Think also of the "Charge of the Light Brigade," which was a battle *lost,* one of the great administrative-command fiascos.

The romance of warfare is not confined in its raw appeal to poets. For instance, the great British biologist-Marxist-pacifist J. B. S. Haldane recalled how trench fighting during World War I was one of the things he'd most enjoyed. There are countless other examples of war's appeal to seemingly *un*warlike people.

Why does so much of man's literature and poetry deal with war if it is not that warfare is intrinsically attractive, romantic, inspiring, and intellectually interesting? Ironically, war's intellectual appeal is precisely what many people—Feeling-type women, in particular—find most distasteful and perverse about it. Feeling-women tend to become profoundly disturbed over war's abstractions, whereas many men absolutely delight in them.

These observations would seem to raise the question, again, of whether man is not by his nature a warring creature, possibly doomed to destroy himself in his genetically predestined pursuit of the delights of warfare. A fair case can apparently be made for this point of view, inasmuch as man has spent the greater part of his collective existence on this planet as a hunter, is a highly territorial creature (particularly in his very early years), is a tool and weapon maker and carrier, is biologically endowed with irritability, and has been subject for most of his days to lethal and debilitating disease, which has made societies short on women from time to time and so led to warring. It does not necessarily follow, however, that a proclivity for warfare is built into man's genes, as some writers suffering *mea culpa* maintain these days.

A much better case can be made for war's being of social utility than for its being man's genetic legacy. Every society, from the tribal level on up, is confronted by the problem of what the elder men are going to do with the young men, who want the women as well as the honor of the group. War helps solve this problem by putting the active and aggressive young men somewhere else. Not only does war transpose the young men, but it permits the society to act out internal tensions, reducing the likelihood that internal violence will erupt.

Some well-balanced societies have worked out these matters quite well, if not completely. Many of the American Indian tribes had programmed a careful progression for their males, starting with the "rank" of baby, then child, boy, young warrior, full brave, chief, then old chief who becomes involved in war but does not engage in battles, then older wise man who does not go to war at all, and, finally, old, old man who serves as the repository of the history of the tribe.

When men send their sons to war, they are in a sense sending themselves to experience once more the perils from which they emerged alive (otherwise they wouldn't be around to send their sons to war). They are also getting rid of some nasty headaches at home. This is not quite so with women, who, by themselves, supply part of the reason for the young men's going off to war. It may be a harsh observation, but as the older gentlemen sigh at the thought of so many young lives being imperiled in a distant war, they may also sigh at "the peace that comes with loved ones far away." With factors such as these *and* the highly romantic qualities of war, we must command a great deal more than sweet reason to find a way around war as a proper occupation for man.

Ideally, as history has shown, a society would like to have not one big, long war to fight but various little wars of reasonably short duration which will not be too costly. The Vietnam War, remember, was once *promoted* by men who eventually opposed it bitterly because it had grown so in size, had lasted "much too long," and had extracted an unconscionable cost in lives, dollars, and goods. As a result, opposition to the Vietnam War grew steadily, and on several occasions produced outbreaks of internal violence in this country.

WARFARE'S APPEAL TO THE FOUR FUNCTIONAL TYPES

As horrible as war can be, it nevertheless seems to have "something for everyone." This means, of course, that any substitute for war will similarly have to have something for everyone, too. This can perhaps best be appreciated if we look at warfare's appeal from the viewpoint of the Typology (see Chapters 2 and 3).

Consider first the Feeling-type, for whom war is one of the great sources of romance, loyalty, treachery, and other strong feelings of all kinds. Any Feeling-type who has been involved in a war and who has had comrades in war is probably very nostalgic over the experience; great perils shared always have a special aura. For people whose sense of romance is strong and whose sense of time lies in powerful feelings of the past, war will provide a constant source of legend: "Old men forget: yet all shall be forgot, but he'll remember with advantages what feats he did that day," as Shakespeare's Henry V says very sensibly, with the analytical detachment of the Thinking man. Moreover, it doesn't matter to the Feeling-type whether a battle or war is won or lost; triumph and disaster are the same to him.

These matters hardly concern the Thinking person. He sees war as the Greatest Game of all. War, after all, is the real thing. Great Thinking men of war have a special respect for one another, no matter the sides taken. The German general Gerd von Rundstedt spoke glowingly of Montgomery and Patton and deeply appreciated their differences. Montgomery, in his writings about warfare, has very carefully rated world military leaders. Concerning Waterloo, he wrote how disappointing it is that the two great generals (Wellington, a Thinking-Sensation-type, and Napoleon, an Intuitive-Feeling-type) each had an extremely bad day. The battle was therefore no test of each one's prowess against the other. Napoleon, it seems, had suffered an attack of hemorrhoids, which gave him such great pain that he did not align his artillery with his usual skill. And the Duke had allowed himself to fall behind in his military duties because he was carrying out other functions, those of a diplomat, among others. Also, he was probably a little under the weather for having attended the Duchess of Richmond's ball the night before.

War is attractive to the Sensation-type because it is immensely ceremonious and loaded with status and hierarchical ramifications that are open to manipulation. War also involves the use of all kinds of marvelous gadgets, devices, and machines and requires the donning of splendid uniforms—all features full of sensations.

For the Intuition-type, certain stages of war offer great opportunities, both for inspiring and for being inspired. If a war hasn't been going on very long, it is *new*, and certain adventures, yet to be tried, are seen as enormously exciting and seductive for the Intuitive, who would like to project into the future and savor the consequences of various hypothetical maneuvers. Clearly, this is a chancy business. Although some Intuitive military leaders are unbelievably successful, most of them are not.

From even this brief analysis of war's appeal to the four functional types, one is forced to the dreadful conclusion that there is *no* chance—certainly not among young males—that war will *not* provide something for everyone. This means that any substitute for war must have something for everyone, and this something must carry almost as strong an appeal as war does itself.

FUNCTIONAL EQUIVALENTS OF WAR

William James long ago recognized the need for "the Moral Equivalent of War," and he would have certainly agreed that to find such a substitute we must look into the whole social psychology and psychophysiology of war and then construct something that will be its functional equivalent without supporting mass violence.

Of course, people have been using functional equivalents of warfare for some time, and with some success. Certain tribes in New Guinea have "wars" that stop the moment someone on either side suffers "injury," which can be as slight as a bruise from being struck with a stick. The young Masai in Africa are fully equipped to fight their human enemies but also fight lions single-handed to show that they are worthy to fight their enemies. In days of old, the young knights would joust in preparation for war, which often did not develop; nonetheless, the young men were *kept occupied* in preparation for it. Young American Indian braves learned to "count coup"—to ride and, instead of killing the opponent, touch him with a finger, showing the height of contempt for the enemy and also the height of courage.

The conservative nature of eighteenth-century warfare provided a perfect stage for Napoleon to display his military prowess. The generals of the early eighteenth century were sensible men. They had suffered the dreadful Thirty Years' War, in which Germany was devastated. The military leaders were fed up with big, long, and costly wars. To replace the deplorable situation of a "nation in arms" they turned to warfare based on maneuver and rules. Another great advantage of the small war of strategy and maneuver was that those who didn't want to participate in it didn't have to.

The American Indian had a similar view of warfare. In Thomas Berger's marvelous book *Little Big Man*, when the great old chief Tent Skins assesses the Indians' great triumph at Little Big Horn, he declares that this is the end of it for the Indians. The Indians were fighting as white men did, under their great war chief, Crazy Horse, and by doing so were destroying their traditional Indian view of war as a dangerous game.

It would seem that a useful course to pursue toward a substitute for war would be to search for a tolerable kind of game which would be no more dangerous than, say, automobile racing; this would allow a few people who wished to do so to take part and, perhaps, to get killed. We might look to something on the order of the famous "Battle of the Thirty," which was fought in the fourteenth century between the English and French when both were running out of juice. They picked thirty champions on each side to battle over possession of a fortress and fought it out under prearranged rules, the French under the great Bertrand du Guesclin, constable of France, finally winning. This "game" avoided depletion of the dwindled resources of the two nations.

This sort of thing would allow young men to engage in exciting activities, poets to write about the tragedy of it all, and those girls who enjoy it to see their boyfriends off on heroic missions.

People will no doubt say that all of this is a lot of blue-sky idealization. Poppycock! Many intelligent men at different periods of history and around the world have undertaken such schemes—and succeeded. Are we such clods that we are less able than the men who built this republic? If we have indeed come down so far in the world we had better work very hard to catch up with our great-great-grandfathers. The alternative is too dangerous.

Changing the Climate for Violence

The question being asked everywhere is: What can be done about violence? There will no doubt be thousands of suggestions. Many of them will either exert their effects very slowly or will be more or less unfeasible. Spiritual revivals, extraordinary as they may be in their effects, are not to be commanded by anyone. I am not sure that this should necessarily be deplored; there are disadvantages, as well as advantages, to spiritual revivals. (Spiritual revivals since Mohammed, Peter the Hermit, the Crusades and Cromwell's Puritans have often been the occasion for an even greater violence than that shown by the nonrevived.)

I believe that it would be feasible to attack this grave problem at two very different levels. The first consists of deploying a series of experiential tests of the sort described in our next chapter. Now that we know the principles involved, with fairly limited resources (and there is no real reason why resources for this should be small) we should be able to develop remarkably effective instruments for exploring the worlds of those who are currently violent and those who might become so.

Once we know how to explore the umwelts of violent people, the possibility for heading off violence becomes something that can be explored. This end of the problem does not seem inherently difficult, even though there may be many practical problems.

Can anything be done about this *climate of violence?* It doesn't seem likely that big changes in mothering or fathering will be made quickly or easily; and even when these occur, they will do little to help our present misfortunes. What we need is a change in fashion.

Dueling was once considered brave, honorable, and the mark of a gentleman, both in Britain and America. Today, dueling would be held barbarous, irresponsible, and, above all, ridiculous. We now look upon it as being the *natural* thing not to duel, whereas dueling was natural and proper among certain classes two hundred years ago. Is there any way of speeding up such a change in climate today?

There is at least one instance in which the behavior of fierce, armed men was transformed greatly within a *very few years.* We know how this was done, and we know who did it. The feat was not completely successful, but we should still be able to learn much from it. The innovator was a remarkable woman, the wife of two kings and the mother of two more. Her name was

Eleanor of Aquitaine. In her own duchy, Eleanor (and her daughters) began to insist that the men at court behave better, and she succeeded. Warriors who reeked of sweat and the stables were encouraged to wash, scent themselves, and become less beastly. They became as much esteemed for decent manners, singing, and dancing as for riding, jousting, drinking, and quarreling. Eleanor's court was imitated throughout Europe.

In this case, the usually silent majority of humankind—women—exerted their influence, powerfully and beneficially. Is that influence any less today? Could it not be mobilized in a good cause?

In our gun-ridden culture (there is said to be up to 200 million guns in the possession of civilians) the majority of the population—women—are not encouraged to carry guns; and they seldom do so, even though this has nothing to do with their physical ability. Modern weapons can be handled well by enough women who, after all, have shown themselves able to handle millions of two-ton weapons (automobiles). Women's lack of interest in guns is curious. According to the early psychoanalytic views, women supposedly suffered from penis envy, and should therefore be very keen about guns. But they are not!

It has been claimed that men enjoy buying, carrying, and using guns in order to impress *themselves*, and no doubt women, too, with their masculinity. However, the nature of masculinity is defined as much by women as by men. Women might therefore mount a sustained and determined attempt to redefine the prestigious masculine persona. This is what Eleanor of Aquitaine and her daughters successfully did. The brawler with a dagger became not manly and brave, but odious and disgusting. This had a remarkable effect on very unruly men almost eight hundred years ago.

Since little boys are much affected by the behavior of older boys and men, it would be best to start the campaign with men. The majority sex must make a sustained, determined, single-minded effort of the same kind that Eleanor and her daughters made, stressing that behavior must change because gun-carrying has become dangerous to society as a whole. The United States is rich in intelligent, well-educated, independent women who support tens of thousands of good causes. Surely there are few more urgent than this one. Women could make the gun-toting male appear not merely unheroic, but impotent, absurd, and, above all, ridiculous. They could then initiate and organize a handing-in of guns and establish rigorous control of those kept for hunting and other purposes. When Eleanor did this with her swordsmen, she in effect redefined the male role.

Has the non-gun-toting majority abdicated its responsibility? In spite of their wealth and numbers (there are more women in the United States and they live longer than men), they have allowed the gun culture to be propagated. Had they attended to this matter as they should have (they are the mothers, sisters, wives, lovers, daughters and grandmothers of every gunslinger, real or fantasied, in this country), they could have done much to reduce these recurring and devastating tragedies. I do not believe that the technique of Lysistrata would have been necessary.

The disarmament of the gun-carrying minority of the United States is really long overdue. Every device of modern persuasion should be used to this end. An Aquitanian or Eleanorian Association could be formed using the talents of such formidable ladies as Margaret Mead, Coretta King, and the women of the Kennedy clan. Collected weapons could be melted and molded into busts of our slain heroes as a reminder of earlier follies. This might civilize us as effectively and as quickly as Eleanor tamed the dung-footed jousters of her day.

8

Exploring the Worlds
of the Mentally Sick

Need for Instruments and Procedures
for Measuring Mental Illness

Clearly, ways must be found to lessen the terrible toll of violence against humanity. *Preventing* violence would, of course, be the most satisfactory solution. One approach to prevention would be, as suggested in the previous chapter, to reduce the availability of the instruments with which so much violence is committed. Even more effective would be the development of means for *anticipating* violence so that it might be headed off by acceptable countermeasures.

As for personal violence, what is needed is a kind of "psychiatric thermometer" that can register the fever of violence before a crisis develops. An instrument of some sort is needed for detecting and measuring violent tendencies in people simply because this cannot be done "by inspection." One often cannot tell merely by watching and listening to him that a potentially violent person harbors violence; chances are that in most cases he will appear normal. Things seem quite turned around when you consider where most of the potentially violent people can be found at any one time (if we know how to find them, that is). They certainly are *not* in our mental hospitals. The great majority of the institutionalized mentally ill are—appearances to the contrary—completely harmless. I would feel safer on the grounds of any mental hospital I know, in fact, than on the streets of many of our major cities—for that is where the majority of our potentially violent people are. Many of them have been in mental hospitals and released, still ill—and dangerous for want of a psychiatric thermometer.

The problem is that, so far, there is no generally accepted way of exploring the world of the mentally sick person quickly and effectively so that one can ask such obvious questions as *how* likely he is to harm himself or others. There are hardly any tests that can be conducted easily and repeatedly so as to *quantify* the danger to himself or others inhering in the sick person.

It is very curious that so little effort seems to have been made to produce adequate psychological instruments and procedures that could be used in everyday work and which would be at least as good as the best clinical opinions.

The usual psychiatrist neither uses tests of this kind nor deplores their absence. He seems simply to be unaware that there might be any other way of coping with this tragic problem. He is, of course, not to be blamed personally for this, but surely psychiatry and psychology as a long-established branch of clinical medicine and a major "scientific discipline" cannot escape censure. More than half a century has gone by during which it has been obvious what is required. Yet, so far as I can make out, the two disciplines have made only the most modest concerted effort toward solving a problem that seems no more difficult than many that have already been solved. It is quite strange that while so much else has been done, this has been neglected. It is impossible to get an answer to the crucial questions: "How ill when he went in?" and "How much better when he came out?"

It is understandable that since no useful answer can be expected from such questions, they are not asked!

After half a century or more, we still do not have usable routine procedures but attempt to inquire into each case of mental illness on its own merits. Of course, at some point in the procedure for each case we have to do this. But adequate tests, properly employed, would allow a much more exact focusing on the "merits of the case" than is possible at present.

A medicolegal report in a book on the Durham rule called *To Make the Mad Guilty* described a case in which a lawyer said with satisfaction—and, indeed, admiration—that, *after at least ten interviews,* a psychiatrist had learned that the patient accused had auditory hallucinations. (The Durham rule discussed the legal responsibilities of mentally disturbed people.) The lawyer apparently considered that this reflected favorably on the psychiatrist's patience and astuteness. If it is necessary to spend that many interviews to gain such crucial information, our battle will often be lost before it has begun.

Psychiatry has few instruments that are widely used and understood and whose value and worth are universally accepted. This is a misfortune. One has only to imagine practicing medicine without a thermometer, a timed quantitative pulse, blood pressure apparatus, and stethoscope. With those three quantitative measures and one qualitative measure, combined with history taking, careful observation of the patient's immediate condition, and a complete physical examination, many useful conclusions about the physical state (and often the mental state) of the individual can be reached. Lacking such instruments, psychiatry is very much in the position of internal medicine in the 1840s, which was most unsatisfactory, as Sir Charles Newman noted in his history of medical education. The clinical test has come a very long way since then.

The routine "test" for anemia in England in the late 1930s was inspection of nail beds, lips, conjunctiva, and other accessible mucous membranes. This is always worth doing, but not as a means of spotting anemia. There are far too many false negatives and some false positives; a hemoglobin analysis tells one so much more. Much the same applies to the chest X-ray, which continued to be looked upon as an adjunct to inspection, percussion, auscultation, and general stethoscope wielding. It is now clear that in many circumstances—particularly when there is evidence of chest illness—a chest X-ray is obligatory. The EEG and the Wassermann test had much the same history.

At present, our clinical procedures in psychiatry for assessing the patient's inner condition are very crude. They are not such that the average psychiatrist can quickly and effectively weigh and correlate the information that he gets at interviews. In addition, there are confounding factors. Older psychiatrists are liable to see wild and woolly boys as being "odd" because of the powerful impact of long hair, beards, and fantastic turnout. This can be of serious consequence for sick boys, for if all the wild and woolly are "unnormal," how does one know who is really ill? "Square" boys, on the other hand, are liable to be seen by the senior psychiatrist as essentially right-minded, conforming, and healthily unimaginative (if the psychiatrist considers those qualities as healthy); they thus tend to have their actual degree of illness *minimized*. I have found no notable relationship between hair length and mental health. Quiet people are easily mistaken for being a good deal healthier than they are. With women, the confounding factor is the overactivity of the schizophrenics, who tend to be seen as sexy, extraverted, naughty but seductive hellers—when they are simply ill.

Perhaps the largest confounding factors are drugs and alcohol, whose presence frequently much reduces the zeal with which the search for schizophrenia is sustained, presumably because of a mistaken economy of hypothesis—a case of cutting one's throat with Occam's razor!

This sort of difficulty has probably existed as long as psychiatry has existed. Class bias in psychiatry, as elsewhere, is always present. But the emphasis on rapid turnover of patient load in many mental hospitals—the "revolving door" policy—has made the matter of the patient's danger to self and to others even more important to detect. It seems likely that the revolving door too often has cut off young lives, of which it can be said in Chidiock Tichborne's tragic lines:

> *The day is past, and yet I saw no sun;*
> *And now I live, and now my life is done.* . . .
> *My fruit is fall'n, and yet my leaves are green* . . .
> *My thread is cut, and yet it is not spun.*

Tichborne's great elegy, written, it is said, the night before his execution for treason (elegy writing was a sensible preexecution habit of Elizabethans), underlines Dr. Samuel Johnson's observation on his forger friend Dr. Dodds, a theologian: "Depend on it, Sir, when a man knows he is to be hanged in a fortnight, it concentrates his mind wonderfully."

A policy that encourages rapid release of patients, plus the use of tranquilizing drugs, makes it easy to suppose that all is well *unless* one knows just how ill the patient was at the time of admission and how much better on leaving.

In addition, there is an effect—how large, I do not know—of the "subpsychiatries," such as those of R. D. Laing, T. S. Szasz, and Eric Berne, which confuse personal fulfillment, civil rights, and game playing with the assessment of grave and sometimes fatal illnesses and so make it even harder for inexperienced young psychiatrists (who naturally want to be in tune with the times) to take a long, cool, detached look at their patients. Clearly, they —most of all—need assistance in assessing the quality and intensity of their patients' mental conditions.

If one can place the beginnings of clinical psychology with Cyril Burt's work in 1918, it seems astounding that more than half a century later psychiatry should be so badly equipped that

—apart from two exceptions to be described presently—the profession has no reliable screening device for spotting mental illness. This deficiency is even more confounding in light of the fact that all the rest of medicine *depends* upon such devices today.

Capping it all is the strange and melancholy fact that not one psychiatrist in a hundred ever complains about the absence of reliable measures; they nearly all accept it with stoicism. Psychologists, too, are remarkably unconcerned with this grave shortcoming of their profession. It is difficult to determine whether the psychological and psychiatric professions are largely *unaware* of the deficiency or are simply *disinclined* to tackle the job of doing something about it. In either case, there seems to be, at root, a failure in theory, combined with a preoccupation with "broad" rather than "deep" approaches to understanding the gravest mental illnesses.

Two Objective Psychiatric Measures: HOD and EWI

The existence today of two objective psychiatric measures of mental illness—the Hoffer-Osmond Diagnostic test (HOD) and the Experiential World Inventory (EWI)—testifies to the effectiveness of the deep approach to probing the worlds of madness.[1] The tests do not attempt to relate influences of society, family, or early sexual experiences to a sick person's mental state; rather, the tests penetrate the person's own umwelt, revealing in simple terms how he perceives the world, other people, himself, and relationships among them all. As will be shown, the tests are

1. A. Moneim El-Meligi and Humphry Osmond, *Manual for the Clinical Use of the Experiential World Inventory* (New York: Mens-Sana Publishing, Inc., 1970); Harold Kelm, "The Hoffer-Osmond Diagnostic Test," in David Hawkins and Linus Pauling (eds.), *Orthomolecular Psychiatry: A Treatment of Schizophrenia* (San Francisco: W. H. Freeman & Co., 1973), pp. 327–41.

remarkably effective in doing what they were designed to do: *measure* mental illness. There are a number of consistency measures in the EWI, but not in the HOD, a much simpler and cruder test. Both EWI and HOD have a high test-retest consistency.

We did not develop the tests deliberately but out of desperation. In the mid-fifties, when we were still working on our theories of schizophrenia, we wanted to test the effect of certain drugs on the illness. Naturally, we wanted to be able to obtain "before" and "after" measures of patients' illnesses so that we could see if a particular drug had actually done anything. This turned out to be impossible with any existing psychological test. Our very able psychologist colleagues devoted at least a year of library work to this problem and eliminated every known test as useless for our purposes. One of the tests eliminated was the Minnesota Multiphasic Personality Inventory (MMPI), which had been developed expressly as a measure of abnormal personality (although it came to be most widely *mis*used to test normal subjects). The famous Rorschach test was also unsuitable, having been developed to study normalcy (but it is often *mis*used to test for pathology). In addition, the Rorschach was far too complicated, requiring three hours to administer and perhaps six hours more to score. By 1960, all available psychological tests had been tried and rejected, including the famous Cattell indexes.

This state of affairs infuriated my colleague, Dr. Abram Hoffer. He couldn't believe that no basic instrument existed of the sort that was absolutely essential to serious psychological and psychiatric research into mental illness. In a cold temper that is characteristic of Abe when he is not suffering fools gladly, he declared that if psychology had not produced the test we needed and was either unable or disinclined to do so, then *we* would make one. And what's more, Abe said, "Our test will be so 'objective' that you will be able to *weigh* the results!"

No psychologist who heard Abe's vow took it seriously, of course. It turned out, however, that his prediction was literally accurate; we often could (we didn't, of course) reach a crude diagnosis of a patient by simply hefting the two stacks of cards he had sorted in carrying out the test.

The HOD test is based on a catalog of experiential changes associated with schizophrenia which we culled from years of written reports by patients and from schizophrenics' literary efforts, such as *The Witnesses*. Development of the HOD and EWI owes a lot, therefore, to the very people they were primarily designed for. We are also indebted to the MMPI and Rorschach and to an excellent questionnaire for determining disability that was devised by the Cornell University Medical School in New York. Our greatest indebtedness, however, is to N. D. C. Lewis and Z. A. Piotrowsky, who first called attention to prognostic factors that were closely associated with schizophrenia.[2] They counted ten such factors in their 1954 paper, and at least five of them were concerned with perceptual disturbances.

In its present form, the HOD consists of 145 cards, a box labeled "True" and a box labeled "False," plus the necessary score forms, keys, and manual. For doctor, nurse, secretary, social worker, or even family member it is very simple to administer. It seldom requires more than fifteen minutes for even the very ill to complete the test; there is no time limit, and, since the HOD is not an intelligence test, there are no "correct" answers, either. The HOD is introduced to patients as a kind of "window" on their experiences so that a better understanding of their affairs can be achieved. Patients seem to like this. Very few refuse to take the test, and patients rarely fake answers; indeed, they seem to sense the value to themselves of complete honesty.

Scoring the test takes only five to ten minutes, depending

2. N. D. C. Lewis and Z. A. Piotrowsky, "Clinical Diagnosis of Manic Depressive Psychosis," in *Depression*, ed. by P. H. Hoch and J. Zubin (New York: Grune & Stratton, 1954), pp. 1–24.

upon the detail required and the skill of the scorer. Interpretation of the result by the clinician takes somewhat longer, but not much. As a rough rule, any total score over 40 in adults is suspicious, and scores over 50 always call for careful scrutiny. Scores well over 100 are not uncommonly registered by seriously ill persons—*even those who have not been previously diagnosed as being ill.* In addition to its diagnostic uses, the HOD seems to possess *therapeutic* value in helping convey to the patient that the doctor is in tune with his world. This aspect of the test was perhaps best evidenced by a sick woman who, when asked what she thought about the HOD after taking it, said, "Why, the son of a bitch who made this up *knows* something about my illness!"

In addition to the total score, which gives a quick though rough-and-ready assessment of the patient's general condition at the time, the HOD provides a "depression score," a "paranoid score," perceptual and thinking scores, and a few special indicators of insight, depression, and self-perception. These last can be used, in specified combinations, to indicate whether the patient is inclined to violent behavior and, if so, whether that violence is likely to be suicidal or homicidal.

The range of perceptions of others and oneself is impressive the moment you admit *distortions* in the perceptual modalities. Among those modalities in perceiving another person are size (relative to others and to the observer), shape (including proportions), color, texture, temperature, halos, aura, flashing eyes, unusual appendages such as tail, horns, hoofs, and other perceptions of animal qualities. Belief as to the nature of the other person can vary a great deal, from his being a "thing" at one end of the scale, to his being an immortal superbeing at the other. Both extremes, incidentally, may involve considerable danger to other people.

Age is another very important dimension and must be related to one's perception of one's own age. The same is true of nationality. If one begins to perceive others as foreign, marked changes in behavior may result. Still another variable that is likely to produce changes in behavior is social status relative to oneself. It may well be that the Napoleons, Jesuses, and Teddy Roosevelts who used to be such notable residents of mental hospitals derived from subtle and little-understood changes in self-perception of the patients in relation to others. The present explanation for this is that it reflects some kind of overcompensation for a deep sense of inferiority; this may be so, but the evidence for it is scanty. The most objectionable aspect of panchreston (explain-all) explanations such as this is that they stifle inquiry by making us suppose that all is already known when it is not.

For example, it is perhaps legitimate to suggest, as some maintain, that mania is the denial of depression, but only if one inquires whether there is any evidence for such an explanation and also provided that one recognizes that this is probably simply an extension of stoic conceptualization of an ideal human being unencumbered by circumstances. In such a philosophy, *all* emotion is an objectionable—or, at best, an unavoidable—weakness. Depression is certainly unpleasant, but most manias are very uncomfortable, too. It is ridiculous to say that the laughter of someone who has been tickled is a denial of depression; the tickling sensation and laughter are obviously enjoyable—at first. Beyond a certain point, the experience becomes less enjoyable. The degree of pleasure or discomfort seems to be determined by the duration and intensity of the tickling. The most gentle tickling, indefinitely prolonged, used to be employed as a torture; very vigorous tickling hurts. The fact that manics can be hostile and anxious does not mean necessarily that their defenses against depression are crumbling. More likely, they've just had enough!

The questions used in the true-or-false card sorting in the HOD test are along the lines of the following:

I feel as if I'm turned to stone.
Time seems to have changed for me.
Time seems to have stopped.
I think I'm someone else.
All colors look very brilliant.
My head seems bigger than before.
I think I've got someone else's body.
I think my body is changing.
When I look in the mirror, I see someone else.
I am worthless, of no importance at all.
Other people look grim.
Other people look like puppets, like paper cutouts, like
   animals, etc.

And so on, for 145 cards. As strange as such statements may seem to a person who is not mentally ill and never has been, a seriously sick person will find many of the cards highly apt descriptions of his inner experience. Often, a nurse or even a secretary administering the test will be able to spot the seriously ill, whose behavior may not suggest grave mental illness at all.

We have tried to gauge the clinical effectiveness and reliability of the HOD—and our more refined experiential measure, the EWI—but are hampered by the absence of any other objective measures of mental illness against which to rate our tests. In one effort at assessment, however, the HOD showed a correlation of 0.85 with the final, clinical diagnosis of the psychiatrist against a correlation of only 0.75 between his own initial and final diagnoses.

Another measure of the tests' effectiveness would be their degree of acceptance in psychiatric practice. While this is growing in the United States and Canada—the tests are beginning to receive formal recognition in courts of law—use of the tests is still quite limited because they represent views that run counter to current psychiatric theories. (More attention will be given to this matter later in the book.)

The Usefulness of HOD and EWI Tests

One measure of an instrument's efficacy is simply whether it works, particularly whether it has demonstrated predictive capability. Such ability was shown for the first time successfully—though with a tragic outcome—some time ago when my colleague Dr. A. Moneim El-Meligi was working on the development of the EWI. A much more powerful, complex, and refined instrument for quantifying experience than the HOD, the EWI is a longer test and is done on a written form instead of with a deck of cards. Dr. El-Meligi would administer his latest version of the EWI to new psychiatric admissions, taking ten or fifteen of them at a time. One day, he noted that a particular woman patient was falling further and further behind her group in filling out the test. When he asked if she were all right, she assured him that everything was "just fine"; and she eventually finished the test after all the other patients had completed theirs. Unavoidably, Dr. El-Meligi did not get around to scoring her test until midmorning of the following day. Immediately he noticed that there were many signs that the woman was deeply depressed, that she would be quite happy to be dead, and that she was, in fact, considering doing harm to herself. Alarmed, Dr. El-Meligi telephoned her ward to warn nurses, only to learn that the patient was not there but had been sent to occupational therapy. When he checked the therapy room and could not find her, a search was started. They found her body later, amid the broken ice at the edge of a frozen pond, drowned.

Since that experience, Dr. El-Meligi has spotted at least a half-dozen other patients with almost identical configurations of symptoms—deep depression, powerful self-destructive urges, lack of hope. Fortunately, in each case he was able to see to it that appropriate protective action was taken in time to prevent another tragedy.

There have been a great many instances in which one would like to have had an HOD (or, much better, an EWI) measure of a person who committed violence against himself or others: Ernest Hemingway, Marilyn Monroe, Sirhan Sirhan, Judy Garland, Lee Harvey Oswald, and Charles Manson are only a few.

The greatest value of measures such as the HOD and EWI is clearly in the field of psychiatry. Because the HOD is quick and easy to administer, it can be of great aid to a busy psychiatrist in emergency situations, such as when a person comes in off the street in an obvious state of grave distress. The rapid, crude assessment that the HOD permits enables the doctor to interrupt the flow of his work briefly to calculate quickly the "emergency" case's test results and, if the results so indicate, explain to the person that the test shows him to be very ill and in need of psychiatric attention. The doctor can then ask if the patient thinks he is well enough to come back as soon as he can be fitted into the doctor's schedule. The patient is usually so delighted by this sort of attention—reassured by the concurrence that he is indeed sick, as he has suspected himself to be—that he will often say he feels well enough to hold on until he can be seen by the doctor. Patients are not unreasonable, even in matters as serious as suicide, and many can be dissuaded from committing violence simply by being convinced that their illness is not going unnoticed and that it will be tended to as soon as possible. If, however, this seems unlikely to relieve a patient, he can be admitted quickly to a hospital for his own—and others'—protection.

An initial HOD-aided diagnosis can have prognostic capabilities if the HOD is administered once, for indications as to the patient's present condition, and again—in the same visit—

for indications as to how things seemed to him earlier when he was at his worst. This will give the physician two reference points from which to establish a direction—toward worsening or toward improving. The great fidelity of recall of one's experiential world—in schizophrenia as in psychedelic drug experiences—makes this so-called retrospective use of the HOD and EWI valid and extremely useful, even if not completely uncontroversial.

One of my colleagues does not use the retrospective method, believing it to be "unscientific." I find it hard to see what is *un*scientific about it. Science, in Herbert Dingle's phrase, is "the rational relationship of the facts of experience." In principle, *all* experience is recollected; there is no way of communicating the "immediate" experience, for the very process of communicating takes a certain amount of time. Nobody objects to psychological tests on the grounds that they are *always*, philosophically speaking (and, of course, neurophysiologically speaking, too), *reminiscences*, but my good colleague shows a certain prudishness about admitting reminiscence of a longer duration.

I suspect that the chief reason for *not* using the retrospective method is that psychologists, like psychiatrists, don't trust their patients. I'm not suggesting that all patients are trustworthy, but most of them are, most of the time, as the success of the moral treatment and countless other efforts of this kind show. We are certainly taking a lesser risk by trusting most of our patients than by not doing so.

Just as a present and a retrospective administration of the HOD or EWI can at the outset give two clinical reference points from which to establish a direction of change—whether the patient is getting worse or improving, and how—periodic use of the tests during treatment can indicate effectiveness of treatment and other aspects of the patient's progress, or lack of it. For example, an initial HOD of 100 compared with a retrospective "worst" score of 150 would indicate that the patient was somehow getting better, though still very sick. Then, if a HOD score of 70 is registered after three months of treatment, the prospects for recovery fairly soon under what would appear to be effective therapy will look quite good. Communicating this good news to the patient—and to his family—can produce an additional salutary effect on the illness. Not only does the patient's morale go up, but he begins to feel that his therapy is the cooperative enterprise that it truly is, and he puts more of his own effort into it, accepting the responsibility that is rightly his.

It is very important in medicine to have responsible patients. One of psychiatry's great difficulties is in accepting the fact that mentally ill persons are not, by definition, irresponsible. Rather, we can *insist* on patients' being responsible for participating in the joint enterprise of therapy. The HOD and EWI can facilitate this participation in the following way.

One of the first benefits of the HOD and EWI is to demonstrate that what seemed previously to be intangible and vague is much less so than the patient had supposed; this is very reassuring. All illnesses are, with few exceptions, vague in their prodromal and early phases. In schizophrenia, this generalization holds true. Generally speaking, in other illnesses the doctor focuses more and more on certain specific symptoms whose importance he explains and which he proceeds to use as pointers toward diagnosis, prognosis, treatment, and recovery. Schizophrenia is not subject to this limiting and explanatory process. On the contrary, it is liable to engulf the whole of the sufferer's personal, family, and social (even political) life. It is made more diffuse, threatening, and uncertain by many current psychiatric strategies.

A patient is comparatively grateful to have, instead of some frighteningly mysterious ailment, a well-known familiar illness because he quite reasonably supposes that doctors know how to handle conditions they have seen before. At least some of the schizophrenic patient's asociality arises from his isolation *inside* what seems to him an unknown and unknowable illness. It seems likely that at least some of the stigma that attaches to schizophrenia derives from the seeming unknowability of the patient's experience. The patient is not absolutely sure that he *is* ill and fears that his experience may be unique. While the HOD and EWI show by implication that his experiences are part of a well-known illness, those treating the patient must make explicit what is implied. If they don't do this, the patient may be too ill to make that quite small leap by himself.

Other areas of psychiatric concern in which the HOD and EWI can be almost uniquely useful include:

Relapse: If a patient who has been improving, by measure of the tests, suddenly is shown by the same tests to take a turn for the worse, his psychiatrist is alerted to watch for a few possible causes: the patient may have stopped taking his prescribed medicine, or the medicine he is taking may be giving him trouble (especially if it is a tranquilizer or a barbiturate), or he may be smoking marijuana or taking some other psychedelic drug, or he simply may be overstimulated, poorly nourished, or enduring some other form of physiological stress.

Stasis: The patient may fail to improve inwardly while showing outward signs of recovery that tend to disarm his doctor, particularly if the patient is hospitalized and pressure is being applied for his release from the hospital; a persistently high HOD score may under these circumstances prevent premature return of the patient into the community during a phase of his illness in which he is a danger to himself or to others.

Recovery: The patient's condition may return within normal limits, and early assessment of this change can prevent needlessly prolonged hospitalization; periodic HOD measures of the patient's condition after his return to the community may serve also to head off relapse and/or support the person psychologically by providing continued objective measures of his mental well-being.

In addition, the HOD, EWI, and other experiential quantifications under development invite use as screening and counseling devices for schools, colleges, industry, and other purposes.

For example, an EWI was run on voluntary and anonymous young men and women who were doing very poorly at a New York college. It revealed that *more than half of them* were obviously ill and condemned merely to totter along academically, doing their best under the most dismal circumstances. It is heartbreaking to see how hard young schizophrenics struggle to get by in college. Many of them do get by. It is almost unimaginably difficult for them. But most simply fall by the wayside. Such an experience is brutal and frequently humiliating. It is happening to students throughout the world today. Without measures of some sort to screen incoming students and spot those with "controlled" mental problems, there is no systematic way of reducing this tragedy, whose effects often extend far beyond the college days.

The general physician should find occasional use for the HOD and EWI, too, for measuring psychologic reactions to hormones and certain other mind-affecting drugs, to prolonged incapacitation (particularly in casts), to heart surgery (which has been reported to have occasionally serious psychiatric complications), and to child delivery.

A most tragic occurrence might have been prevented, for instance, had a measure been made of the experiential world of a young farm woman. She had given birth to a beautiful baby and then dashed its brains out on a barn door because she thought someone had substituted a pig for her baby. Afterward, no amount of consoling could do much to alleviate the terrible psychic pain that the young woman suffered—and will suffer all the rest of her days, even though she is able intellectually to accept the fact that she wasn't truly "responsible" for her act.

(The potential value of HOD and EWI screening for the identification of alcoholics and drug addicts who have underlying schizophrenia has been noted in Chapter 6.)

PERCEPTUAL MATURATION IN YOUNG PEOPLE

Measures of persons' experiential worlds have given new insight into such matters as perceptual maturation in young people and changes in mood and functional ability associated with menstruation in women.

For many years, the age at which one was generally thought to become an adult was twenty-one. Recently, however, the voting age in the United States was reduced to eighteen. The apparent reason was political in response to the growing potential voting population of Americans between eighteen and twenty-one. Proponents of change argued that our young people are maturing earlier now than they did years ago. Physiologically, this seems to be so: boys and girls get bigger faster than they used to and reach puberty sooner. But one wonders whether these are appropriate measures of change on which to base a revision of the voting age. Our studies of the perceptual maturity of young men and women raise additional questions on this score.

Just before I left Weyburn Hospital in Saskatchewan, in 1961, we ran HOD tests on the young people who had come to help out during the summer. We were alarmed to find that many of them tested very strange indeed. This led Dr. Hoffer to set up a serial test of youngsters as they progressed through school in Saskatchewan.

He found that children of, say, thirteen, show far more perceptual anomalies than the same ones show at sixteen. They show even fewer perceptual anomalies when they are eighteen, and still fewer when they are about twenty-one. Boys seem to stabilize at around twenty-one; girls, at about twenty-three. Both sexes finally settle down to the stable world of adults, becoming, you might say, as dull as the rest of us.

What this indicates is that while today's eighteen-year-old may be physically, physiologically, or sexually more mature than yesterday's was, he or she is still not fully mature perceptually —or experientially. It is important to remember, in this connection, that one's perceptual and other inner experiences can often affect one's judgment and behavior.

Nevertheless, current sentiments support claims, based upon very modest and questionably relevant evidence, that eighteen-year-olds today are in some way more enlightened than they were, say, twenty years ago. We have no idea whether they are or not; yet we have changed the voting age to satisfy these sentiments. Somehow, it seems that more than sentiment should be required before handing out votes, particularly when one should realize that eighteen-year-olds of today are much more numerous proportionately *and* more likely to be adolescent than those of a hundred years ago, when many of them had been in the working world for six years or more.

Most peculiar of all is the fact that the very members of "the establishment," who fought for the eighteen-year-old vote, wished also to stamp out psychedelic drug use at a time when a growing proportion of the young voters is pressing for legalization of marijuana! One wonders if these men have decided to retire from politics in some subtle way.

CHANGES ASSOCIATED WITH MENSTRUATION

HOD and EWI studies appear also to have something to say about the liberation of women, if in a rather roundabout manner. Our evidence strongly suggests that the menstrual cycle is accompanied by perceptual and mood changes that can occur either together or separately. This suggestion may be important, since it has a bearing on at least half the world's population for a considerable part of their lives. Just what proportion of that population is affected in this way and to what extent they are distressed remains to be seen.

In recent years, we have had another factor introduced: the Pill. Are those who normally have premenstrual perceptual oddities more or less likely to have them after taking the Pill? What will be the consequences for women who take the Pill plus some other medication, such as weight-control substances and treatments for asthma and allergies?

Many complex drug reactions involving perceptual disturbance are quantifiable with tests like the HOD and EWI, which would also facilitate monitoring the modification of these experiential drug reactions medically.

Such matters may seem to be of limited and special interest only, but they are actually extremely important. It is well known, for example, that women—who tend to be "acriminal" on the whole—incline toward crimes of violence and theft (shoplifting, particularly) during the menstrual period. Another important factor is that the perceptual and mood anomalies that women experience at this time are often a source of great fear and worry to them. It may well be that this is one of the underlying reasons why many women seem less than enthusiastic about members of their sex entering politics—knowing their own fears and worries, they may wonder whether a female political leader might not err unfortunately if she became perceptually unstable at a critical moment in public life.

But there is another side of this coin, too. Male politicians appear certain of their rockbound stability that they will carry on in political crises—even when they are three-quarters dead. Women politicians might actually be a good deal safer. They are accustomed to periodic bouts of temporary instability—

mostly inconsequential—and are quite able to admit when they are not "100 percent." In this way, the menstrual cycle may eventually play a large and crucial role in the ultimate liberation of women.

SUICIDE OF THE YOUNG

Press headline: "Suicide Is Found 2d as Cause of Death among Collegians."

It seems that information about some matters seeps only slowly through our profession—e.g., the high rate of suicide among young schizophrenics. Many of them are intelligent and go to college. Usually their college is large, impersonal, bureaucratic, and far from their homes—about the worst possible environment for them.

Another aspect of schizophrenia has also received scanty attention. The menarche in girls has been occurring earlier for the last forty to fifty years at least. There has been no agreed-upon explanation for this, as far as I know. Boys and girls have become healthier and taller, and they mature sexually earlier in a society that tries to postpone adult status longer and longer. This in itself is a curious and paradoxical business. With our usual pigheaded lack of observation, we have paid little or no attention to changes in the most immediately accessible parts of our environment, our bodies.

If schizophrenia has a biological basis, it seems at least likely that earlier maturation (biologically) will be accompanied by earlier schizophrenia. If so, this will not only present itself in an unfamiliar manner but probably will have different consequences. The illness will occur in a population with fewer acquired social skills and less sense of solidarity with the adult world—thus rendering the potential victims even more vulnerable.

When considered in this way, schizophrenia appears likely to become an even more potent killer of the young. This view emphasizes the value of a means for identifying potential suicides and heading them off, as is possible with the HOD, the EWI, and similar devices.

SEXUAL MATTERS

Sexual problems are today considered to be an essential feature of grave psychiatric illness, just as seventy-five years ago religious problems were usually assigned a large place in grave mental illness. At the turn of the century, loss of faith, an increase in religious enthusiasm, and concern with novel and unfamiliar kinds of religion were considered to be of great importance and were recorded carefully in psychiatric notes. Today comparatively little attention is paid to such matters, while sex has a great fascination for both patients and their psychiatrists. I suspect that patients who complain of impotence or failure to achieve orgasm receive far more sympathetic and concerned attention today than those who complain of loss of faith. Yet, it is a matter of personal preference; which misfortune should one consider the graver? It would require empirical studies to determine how many people consider one, both, or neither of these views catastrophic.

What effect would one expect grave misperceptions to have upon sexual relationships? Ideal sexuality is a physical, emotional, and spiritual relationship. Popular (or unpopular) sex books and articles seldom recommend that young people of either sex who wish to be initiated into the art should hire the services of an adept professional who would teach them all about it. Such a viewpoint has, however, been held by people of profound sensibility. Charles James Fox's father, the corrupt but lovable Lord Holland, procured a mistress for young Charles when he was fourteen. Charles remained deeply attached to her throughout his life, which included a remarkably happy marriage. Under his father's kind tutelage, Charles grew up to be one of the very few eighteenth-century politicians in England who could not be bought—the more remarkable since his father had the reputation of being the most corrupt paymaster general in England's history.

In our culture, sexuality is acquired by do-it-yourself learning. One would suppose that being able to perceive oneself and one's sexual partner—and the relationship between the two—would be very important for any mutually satisfying sexual relationship. The more enduring this relationship is, the more essential it is that there be no great perceptual discrepancies. Indeed, much marriage counseling is aimed at reducing these mutual misunderstandings. If one's HOD score is over 100, the chances are remote that one will have a stable and appropriate self-perception or that one's perception of others will be steady. Yet, unless one can rely upon these essential perceptual cues, it is hard to see how one can behave appropriately so as to initiate, develop, and sustain an appropriate relationship.

Perceiving oneself or others as animals, or animals as humans, has many kinds of predictably unfortunate consequences. Some of them depend upon the kind of animals one perceives oneself and others to be and how one feels about them. The literature of witchcraft is replete with examples of sexual relationships between people and imaginary beings, such as devils, succubi, incubi, and even angels. It is also rich in tales of sexual relations with a great variety of animals frequently held to be agents of the devil.

It is a matter of debate whether a more permissive sexual climate would help or harm schizophrenics. An atmosphere in which there is minimal guilt, shame, and fear about sex should help schizophrenics to the same extent that it helps those who are not afflicted in this way. At the same time, self-esteem has come to be much more closely linked to acknowledged sexual success than it was fifty to a hundred years ago. Thus, one result of making sex more discussable will be to lower the self-esteem of those who fail in this way.

Sex always has been discussed, of course, but it is now far more obligatory to talk of it than used to be the case. People now out-wardly expect—even demand—much more in the way of sexual satisfaction than they used to. Just as healthy-minded people seventy or eighty years ago were expected to have certain fairly predictable *religious* interests, so it is with sex today. Those who lacked religious zeal were usually exhorted to develop it by study, prayerful exercises, confession, penances, even exorcism. The mentally sick person today considers that sex is bound to be a matter of central importance; the psychiatrist or other psychotherapist feels bound to prescribe a suitable regimen.

In the early days of psychoanalysis, the regimen was almost always continence, which suggests that earlier attitudes and values were still working. Things are often very different today. Some analysts have been reported as advising a "therapeutic" affair. Others apparently advocate, "under certain circum-stances," sexual relations of a therapeutic kind *with the analyst.* It is not clear to me how an analyst or other psychothe*rapist* would qualify as a specialist in this field; possibly the examining body should include a knowledgeable madam or pimp.

Sex, with its mystery and magic, has been considered a specific for all kinds of illness. At one time, sleeping with a virgin was held to be a specific treatment for chronic gonorrhea. Sex has also been considered *harmful* in many illnesses and has been held to be the cause of some. In schizophrenia, the central problem is to ensure that the sexual situation and the complex social rela-tionships that attend even casual sexuality are not of a kind that do grave harm to the patient and his or her sexual partner. HOD and EWI findings give *prima facie* evidence that much greater dangers in this respect exist for schizophrenics than for others. Doctors prescribe moderation in many delightful activities in order to speed recovery and prevent more serious illness. It seems to me that sex may be another matter worthy of moderation for schizophrenics.

BEHAVIORAL THERAPY: AVOIDING UNNECESSARY FAILURE

Mr. T., when twenty-five years old, was diagnosed as schizophrenic by the U.S. Army in 1965 and was twice admitted to a V.A. hospital with that diagnosis. After his honorable discharge from the army, he obtained a degree at Brooklyn College, but his life became increasingly seclusive and he was assailed by many kinds of perceptual disturbances. During a two-year psychoanalysis, he seemed to have got gradually worse; he became impotent and preoccupied with homosexuality (which was not wholly surprising, inasmuch as he was told by his analyst that his illness, schizophrenia, was caused by latent homosexuality). Mr. T. even visited a homosexual prostitute, but was impotent.

When his analysis ended, Mr. T. spent six to eight weeks in a V.A. psychiatric hospital and came out on very substantial doses of a strong tranquilizer, Thorazine. His second stay in a V.A. hospital occurred in mid-1971 (after a brief but disastrous return to his native country in eastern Europe, where he stayed three days before fleeing back to New York). In the V.A. hospital he was kept on large doses of Thorazine while undergoing "behavioral treatment" for his impotence and homosexuality. Treatment consisted of administration of an electric shock when male nudes were projected on a screen before him and a pleasurable reward of some sort when female nudes were projected.

Treatment produced no change in Mr. T. As long as he took Thorazine, however, it is doubtful that treatment would have, even if it could have; the behavior therapists seem to have reduced further their already slim chances of success by not concerning themselves with their patient's experience. Mr. T.'s

HOD test was well over 100, which is the equivalent of a moderate trip on LSD or a mild delirium, even though he was still on Thorazine. Since Thorazine tends to make learning difficult, and the patient's perceptual disorders would undoubtedly interfere with his perception of himself and of the female nudes that were being projected on the screen, it seems unlikely that the behavioral conditioning would help him. While these behavioral techniques have much to offer to some sick people, one hopes that those who use them will teach their neophytes not to employ them when such major pharmacological and perceptual variables as those described here make success very unlikely.

PENOLOGY

C. H. Rolph, in an extremely intelligent article written with sanity, detachment, and evident solid knowledge, notes an extraordinary but apparently little-known fact: Out of every 100 men and women sentenced as "first offenders" (this really means offenders *caught* for the first time), 85 do not come back for more punishment, whatever kind of sentence they get. You can fine or imprison them, send them to Borstal or detention centers, discharge them conditionally or absolutely, put them on probation for one, two, or three years, bind them over to keep the peace or to be of good behavior—and the effect will be statistically the same. In November 1960 a prison medical officer wrote that "about the same proportion of newcomers to prison, roughly 85 percent is never sentenced again, as in the days of the broad arrow and the shaven head."[3]

Rolph considers that only 15 percent of the prison population are intractable and dangerous. He writes: "And among that remaining 15 percent [two-thirds] should be under medical care in clinical conditions, rather than in prisons where their treatment is little more than a gesture."

3. C. H. Rolph, *Journal of the Royal College of Physicians of London*, pp. 306–310, Vol. 1, No. 4, July 1967.

It seems likely that using the HOD and EWI would quite easily screen out Rolph's 10 percent who are sick. The 5 percent of "intractables" would, of course, be immediately recognizable once the 85 and 10 percent have been removed. They would also, I suspect, be much more susceptible and vulnerable to being alienated from the criminal subculture to which many of them belong. They would no longer be high-status members of the prison culture, able to bully the 85 percent of single offenders (the one-timers) and the 10 percent of sick people. What the prison system in England—and in the rest of the world—seems to be doing is to provide settings for professional criminals and for members of the criminal subculture to maintain their status and identity.

Sentimentality and sloppy thinking contribute to the stupid way in which prison inmates are handled. As the prison officer notes, things have not changed since the days of the broad arrow. It appears probable that his 85 and 10 percent are much the same from country to country. It should be relatively easy to identify these different populations, separate them, and treat them appropriately.

Why have we failed to do so? Apart from the sluggishness of lawyers, penologists, and the public, I suspect that lack of a usable, quantifiable classification system plays a large part. At present we are not forced to ask and to answer the tricky questions that would make us see the whole problem in a different light. The three populations described by Rolph sound quite easily delineated and so can be separated by studying their umwelts. They are:

1. People who identify with the larger culture but have lapsed (the 85 percent who will not return to prison).
2. Psychotic and neurotic patients, not recognized as such, combined with some labeled psychopaths or "sociopaths," some of whom are certainly psychotic (10 percent).

3. Members of one or more criminal subcultures who are not simply lapsing as in (1) or sick as in (2), but should be considered as dangerous "prisoners of war," requiring indoctrination in societal ways (5 percent).

This 5 percent or so ought to be of central concern to us once we have recognized the dyshomogeneity of the criminal population. Once we understand their sociocultural umwelts and their typology, we are faced with moral and ethical questions, and these ought to be debated.

First, there seems little doubt that we, as members of the larger culture, have both the right and the duty to hamper and, if possible, prevent recruitment to the criminal subcultures. We cannot do this without knowledge. It seems likely that all or most of the necessary facts have long ago been gathered, though not ordered and coordinated, to reach an agreed hypothetical goal of "crime prevention."

Second, our right to prevent ourselves from being victimized by members of the criminal subcultures has long been recognized by custom and law. It seems unlikely that even truly professional criminals are at odds with this notion.

Third, our right to try to change values and attitudes of the criminal subculture through the use of pharmacological knowledge seems to be questionable and requires much further thought. Persuasion in the past has been of a rigorous kind (flogging, the pillory, racking, pressing, thumbscrewing, etc.). We are naturally confident that we will never do anything so barbarous again, although the basis for this confidence seems obscure. (We have daily examples from all over the world that many people prefer the older days because of belief in the efficacy of the methods employed then. Interrogation procedures do not, in fact, seem to have altered much over the centuries, except in the amount of overt violence against the interrogatee that is allowed.) It is undeniable, however, that today we have either available or possible a large number of very powerful techniques—ranging from psychosurgical to psychedelic and hypnotic—for "indoctrination." The questions are: Would it be good to use them? If so, which ones should we use, under what circumstances, and with what safeguards? As usual, writers are well ahead of the game: *Brave New World, 1984, Animal Farm,* and *A Clockwork Orange* are excellent books for those who wish to ponder these aspects of the future.

9

Understanding People in
Groups: Typo-Methectics

Have you ever described the behavior of a seemingly sane, sensible, and sober person as "outrageous"? Have you ever thought in retrospect of your *own* behavior: "I must have been out of my *mind*" to have said or done a particularly beastly thing to someone who didn't really deserve it—a dear friend, a family member, your host, a guest, your employer, an employee, a fellow worker?

To behave strangely—even violently—one doesn't have to be insane, feverish, drunk, starving, menstruating, taking hormones or other mood- or mind-affecting pharmaceuticals, or high on psychedelic drugs or narcotics. Of course, any of those factors can contribute to a person's acting oddly by making him operate under the handicap of distorted perceptions of himself, of others, and of events in the world about him. But distorted perceptions are obviously not the only route to strange behavior.

Faulty Perspective in Human Relationships

When normal, well-adjusted persons suddenly adopt behavior that others (and probably later they themselves) regard as odd, inappropriate, or offensive, the trouble probably lies *not* with faulty perception but with *faulty perspective*.

A person can easily lose perspective in human relations in two ways. First, he can disregard differences in personal points of view of other persons and try to impose his own viewpoint upon them—forcibly, if he feels it is necessary. Suppose two individuals are united in a common cause and want to settle upon a strategy for pursuing their mutual goal. Suppose, also, that one is a future-oriented visionary and the other a present-rooted, "now" sort of person. Obviously, the visionary is unlikely to move the project forward if he tries to impress his colleague with the theoretical, long-range, blue-sky benefits of a particular approach. And the "now" person is not likely to inspire the visionary with the technical details of what he sees to be the most effective, practical, *immediate* approach to the project. Behaving in these ways, the two would almost certainly seem a little "weird" to each other.

The other way in which people most commonly lose perspective in their relations with others is by failing to take proper stock of the distribution of roles, rights, and duties of persons with whom they are engaged, thus precipitating conflicts of authority within a group which interfere with the group's functions. This sort of thing can happen in any group—family, social, business, political, military, etc.

My earliest recollection of being aware that there were different kinds of authority among which conflicts could arise if care wasn't taken occurred during World War II when I was in medical school. The word came down from Whitehall that all medical students were to join the Home Guard to protect the country against invasion. We were all distressed by this news. We had done a good deal of extracurricular rescue work at the hospital during the heavy blitzes of late 1940 and 1941, and we did not want to lose more time to nonmedical activities. We wanted to get through our final exams as soon as possible because we'd eventually have to go into the armed services and we wanted to be as useful *medically* as possible. Besides, our entry into the Home Guard would be coming at a time when the battle had shifted to Russia! To top it off, we learned that the Home Guard was moving into the area of new weapons and wouldn't actually need us at all. We sent in a reply that we did not intend to comply with the order and would push on with our medical studies instead.

An interesting, if rather bizarre, situation ensued. Some of our senior teachers felt that our defiance should not go unpunished and proceeded to make very serious threats to us. They did not take account of two factors, however. The first was that they were threatening intelligent, well-informed people who happened also to be patriotically inclined, having already done a very decent job of rescue in the air raids. The other factor was that our senior teachers had no right to threaten to punish us because they lacked *authority* over the disposition of medical students in this situation. When the matter was taken to senior civil servants at Whitehall—where such authority did reside—the whole problem was put to rest, and we were spared both punishment and stints in the Home Guard.

The two defects in perspective—the disregard of differences in others' viewpoints and the failure to assess roles, rights, and duties properly—often work together against one's own better interests and those of one's associates. In most cases, problems in perspective develop insidiously; many times the individuals involved are not aware that anything is wrong until long after the fact, if then. There seems to be a good reason for this. A person may realize (though many do not) that different people have different ways of looking at things; he may also realize that hierarchies of authority, roles, rights, and duties exist and must be paid attention to in human relations. But without a *system* for the constructive application of this knowledge, perspective on human relationships can be lost or seriously distorted, often with grievous consequences. Until now, no such "system of human relations" existed. Following is a description of one which, though still undergoing development, has already been applied effectively in several formal situations and has shown great usefulness in everyday human affairs.

A Theory of Group-Member Relations: Typo-Methectics

The system is called typo-methectics because it combines features of our Typology (Chapters 2 and 3) and of the theory of methectics. This theory was named after the Aristotelian *methexis* (meaning participation) by its innovator, my old friend and colleague T. T. Paterson, professor of industrial administration at the University of Strathclyde in Glasgow, Scotland. Methectics is a theory for dealing in a practical way with human enterprise in terms of bestowed or adopted roles of members of a group—ergo, *group participation*.

Paterson distilled twenty-five years of well-knit theorizing, keen observation, and elegant experiment in producing his methectics theory. His professional background was in chemistry, geology, and human biology at Edinburgh University, then psychology and anthropology at the University of Cambridge, where he was a fellow of Trinity College and director of the University Museum of Anthropology. He has taken part in several anthropological expeditions to the Arctic, where he studied the use of authority among the Eskimos, and to Africa and northern India. He served in all three British armed forces—as a lieutenant colonel in the Royal Army, a commander in the Royal Navy, and a wing commander in the Royal Air Force—where he carried out experiments in the management of men. Later, he undertook extensive studies of human relations in coal mines and factories. It was in connection with the administrative muddle I found at Weyburn Hospital in Saskatchewan that I became acquainted with Paterson's management theories, and applied them to good effect.

Stated very simply, methectics theory concerns the assignment, adoption, recognition, and execution of forms of authority, roles, rights, and duties of persons engaged in enterprises of various sorts. Methectics addresses itself to participation in the functions of small groups. Underlying Paterson's theory is the rationale that if a group is to survive, it must be able to maintain itself in the face of outside pressure, resist disruptions from within, exact loyalty from its members, establish a system of principles (morality), and adapt to new happenings. There are five major roles in a group, and these are filled most effectively by different people so that each can expand his particular function to the utmost. Once these roles are filled, other group members either understudy them or follow their lead. Paterson summarized the thinking underlying the general scheme of methectics in this way:

It is necessary for every person to express his unique personality. . . . We can express our personality most intensively only when we are with the people with whom we feel compatible, or when we see some reflection which satisfies us, and we need it. Every one of us—as a "new boy" [on the block]—has felt the loneliness of being outside a group (an "isolate") and, willy-nilly, we attempt to get accepted into a group where we can rid ourselves of this loneliness and become "one of the boys."

A group which forms . . . for the purposes of satisfaction of personality needs may thereafter assume another purpose. For example, on the work floor [of a factory], such a group might . . . challenge . . . the manager on a matter of principle concerning wages and conditions. . . . It might even force an argument with the trade union if the members believe they are getting a raw deal. Immediately . . . the group's purpose is no longer only unconscious or subconscious satisfaction of personality needs, but becomes more explicit; the functions become clearer and so do the structure of the functions. Because there are functions and a structure, there must be roles;

hence, according to the personalities of the members making up the group, there is expected role behavior which the role takers adopt. If they do not adopt this role behavior, they [will] not be assigned the functions.

Authority goes with these roles, [administrative] authority because there is a common purpose, and [knowledgeable] authority because of the need for comparative expertness in these functions. A group does things by action, hence there must be "entitlement to do" [rights] vested in those who lead in decisions on action and in those who have the knowledge required for conclusions prior to the decisions. In informal groups, if a person undertakes a function [duty] assigned by the rest of the group and adopts the role behavior appropriate to that function, he becomes entitled [has the right] to act in accord with the authority . . . that goes with that function [duty]. Thus different types of leaders emerge.[1]

Before considering the different kinds of authority, it might be useful to untangle the confusion that seems to prevail over the concepts of authority, on the one hand, and power, on the other.

Power is often spoken of as synonymous with rights. This is a mistake, for legitimacy is implied. The only power that can be said to be truly legitimate is the power that a person with vested authority has to require obedience to his authority. Power can be used to "seize power" (usually illegitimately). As soon as power is seized, however, the seizer rushes to legitimatize himself with authority.

Power, therefore, is a transient thing because one doesn't want to exercise power for very long; he wants to convert it to authority. The reason for this is that power alone is unworkable. One cannot get even slaves to do things unless the slaves are agreeable, and it is authority, not power, to which agreement is secured. It is a great misunderstanding to suppose that the world

1. T. T. Paterson, *Management Theory* (London: Business Publication, Ltd.), 1966.

is governed mostly by power, for it is actually run mostly by authority. This makes one wonder what can be expected from all the movements for "power" of various sorts—black, green, gay, women, youth, and so on. In a very real sense, all those power-seeking centers already *have* power; what they really want is authority. In most instances in which such groups make "power plays" for authority (whether or not they realize that this is what they are really after), using their power is probably not a particularly good way of getting it. Only tyrants and the grossest dictators use power to seize political power (which they convert quickly to legitimatized authority). The most successful of today's power-seeking "out" groups are actually trying to acquire *legitimacy*, which implies role recognition and, hence, authority.

How one goes about acquiring authority most effectively depends, in many cases, upon the *kind* of authority one wants. Paterson concluded early in his studies of group relations that authority is not homogeneous. That is, there is no such thing as Authority-with-a-capital-A that gets divided up among members of a group. Authority comes in several forms, all of which are represented in the roles assumed in group relationships. This means that authority, in its different forms, is a shared quality; all persons in a group possess it, even those who "merely" follow and do not lead. Without the authority of followers, there would be no one to confer authority of leadership upon the leaders.

PRINCIPAL KINDS OF AUTHORITY

Paterson identified five principal kinds of authority in his original theory, and my present colleagues and I have helped him add one more (Aesculapian authority). Very briefly, they are:

Structural authority: the entitlement (right) to command that is *vested in a position* in an enterprise (and so in the person occupying that position) for ordering and coordinating functions pertaining to other positions, and to expect and even require obedience in the ordering and coordinating. In other words, Structural authority constitutes the conferred right to command and to expect and enforce obedience. This is what we usually refer to as administrative or "top" authority.

Sapiential authority: the entitlement to be heard by reason of knowledge, experience, or expertness that is *vested in the person.*

Moral authority: the entitlement to control and direct by reason of "rightness" and "goodness" in action, as judged by members of the enterprise. Hence, this is *vested in the person.*

Personal authority: the entitlement to control and/or direct that is *vested in a person* by reason of fitness of personality, for the purpose of the enterprise, and good fit with the personalities of the other members of the enterprise.

Charismatic authority: the entitlement to control, direct, and/or be heard that is *vested in the person* because he possesses a special, almost indefinable quality that inspires, awes, thrills, attracts, and commands respect and adherence—a kind of "grace."

Aesculapian authority: the very special entitlement to control, direct, and be heard that is *vested in the physician* by virtue of the moral goodness, esteem, and charisma that comes to him "from on high" through his healing ability. ("Honor a physician with the honor due unto him for the uses which ye may have of him: For the Lord hath created him. For of the most High cometh healing . . ." *Ecclesiasticus.*) The charismatic aspects of Aesculapian authority derived from the mystery of both health and illness.

Paterson began developing his theory of authority in the early 1950s and struck almost immediately upon the revolutionary concept of Structural authority—a *position* that has certain rights and duties that can be defined without the presence of a person. Structural authority is a total abstraction, for it does not require a person. By the same token, the rights and duties of persons under a particular Structural authority can be related in a purely abstract way. This is not true of any other kind of authority. While Structural authority is usually the "top authority," it is nevertheless limited in time or in degree or by the existence of other Structural authorities that impinge. Even the president of the United States—probably the greatest Structural authority figure in the world, in many ways—is limited by very substantial and clearly defined constraints upon him. Obviously, the president has no authority to chop off the head of any citizen who makes nasty faces through the White House gates, nor has he authority to chop down the authority of the other two branches of government, though he may exert considerable influence over them in one way or another.

But very little of the everyday affairs of human beings is concerned with Structural authority. Most of the time we are so little aware of Structural authority that we sometimes have great difficulty in recognizing it. We recognize the president and our boss, of course. But most of the time the person who is president or boss commands less attention than the position he occupies. In a sense, Structural authorities tend almost to become "things," and people generally are inclined to reject things for *feelings*. A system under Structural authority must somehow respond to the *feeling* of the people if it is to work. This suggests immediately that there must be another kind of authority in addition to Structural that involves expression of feelings and judgment by people. Such authority would have to be vested in a person and not abstractly in a position.

The first of the "person-centered" authorities that Paterson described is Sapiential, so named because it derives from a person's real or supposed knowledge. This is a very broad form of authority which can, in certain instances, supersede all others (and in some cases *ought* to, but doesn't). Suppose you are the universe's leading authority on public lavatories. You may be quite unable to *order* people around in matters concerning public lavatories, but you may be sure you will be *heeded* by those who need expert guidance in the field, purely because of your expert knowledge of it. You will probably even be invited to attend congresses to display your expertness. Recognition of your great knowledge may earn you the position of director of your own public lavatory, where you *can* order your subordinates around. Being the greatest public lavatory authority, however, has nothing to do with your authority as lavatory director, which is Structural authority. Your expertness—Sapiential authority—inheres in you. When you are promoted to a higher position or decide to leave and become a theoretician on public lavatories, the person who takes on your old position assumes your Structural authority—but he doesn't acquire your Sapiential authority; that goes with you. It belongs to you, and there is no way of getting it away from you.

An illustration of the power of Sapiential authority in the face of "top" authority took place when Leo Szilard and Albert Einstein went to the highest Structural authority in the land. Their expertise resulted in President Roosevelt's initiating the project that produced the atomic bomb, altering the course of history.

Persons who have no claim to expertise and who do not possess Structural authority may, nevertheless, exercise authority of another sort. Paterson enjoys telling the story about the Englishman on holiday in one of the western isles of Scotland. Wanting to post a letter, the visitor found the mailbox enveloped in a canvas cover which was held in place by a padlock. It was Sunday; a sign nearby indicated that mail was to be picked up from the box on Sundays at 4:35 P.M. With the box covered, however, he couldn't put the letter into it. A postman happened by, and the Englishman asked why the box wasn't open. The postman replied, "It's the Sabbath." "Well," said the Englishman, pointing to the sign, "the postmaster general says the post will go at 4:35 P.M. on the Sabbath." The postman responded, "And the minister says that on the seventh day I shall do no work, as the Lord has told us, and here in the islands, it's the Lord's wishes that count."

Quite clearly, the Structural authority of the postmaster general did not hold sway in matters that concerned the religion or morality of the islanders. And it was not the expertness of either the minister or the postman that gave their stand the day. Their position won out because they were voicing the *morality* of the islands; Paterson called this type of authority Moral authority.

Moral authority is important because it reflects how people feel about particular things and their degree of commitment to them. Moral authorities are singularly interesting people. They are usually rather unspectacular, but what they can do better than anyone else is speak from the heart of the entire group. They do not reach conclusions hastily and often take a great deal of time tuning into the moral climate. The person with Moral authority is not, therefore, a front runner, but is usually found in the midst of the group, listening to what people are thinking about and how they are feeling.

General Eisenhower was one of our great moral leaders; indeed, in the view of his friend and critic, and difficult subordinate, Viscount Montgomery, he was probably the only man who could have held warring generals, admirals, and air marshals together as he did in World War II. A formidable man, Ike was also surprisingly unspectacular and even quite dull in comparison to many of his more colorful subordinates.

In addition to Moral authority, Ike possessed Structural authority and Sapiential authority, of course, and the list's fourth type of authority, Personal. Personal authority derives from a person's own qualities—intelligence, strength, beauty, daring, adroitness, wealth, etc.—which are particularly suited to the group and/or the enterprise it is engaged in.

One is reminded of another J. B. S. Haldane story which he used in reply to eugenicists who felt it would be good for the species if we were to get rid of dull people. Haldane said this view would require much thought because a situation could be imagined in which a dullard would actually be the leading authority. He then described a group of five men, four of whom are professors—none weighing more than 150 pounds—imprisoned in a cave by a huge boulder blocking the entrance. The fifth man is a muscular, 400-pound dullard. Under these circumstances, who will have the greatest Personal authority?

Charismatic and Aesculapian forms of authority are closely related to—and may even be considered special kinds of—Personal authority. Charismatic authority is a kind of "magic" Personal authority that attaches to an individual because of certain indescribable qualities he or she possesses; it can become augmented in a position of special prominence, such as the office of the president or the skipper of the national contender in the America's Cup yachting race. Charismatic authority is often as unpredictable as it is magical. Hitler's Charismatic authority successfully infected the German people with his dismal vision and brought about the Second World War. Lincoln, on the other hand, was not always able to work his Charismatic magic. He could not inspire the American people with his benign vision of amortizing the abolition of slavery over the succeeding forty years. Had the President's proposed constitutional amendment been adopted in 1861, all slaves would have been freed by 1900 and the slave owners paid off (emancipation compensation), and a costly and bloody war that literally tore the nation apart would certainly have been avoided.

Aesculapian authority is invested almost as much in the *position* of physician as in the *person* who occupies it. And to a great extent it derives from the eyes of the beholder—usually the patient or, simply, the nondoctor (although doctors can also have Aesculapian authority in their associations with one another). This form of authority is compounded of Sapiential and Moral authority, and it accepts grafts of Charismatic authority if the doctor possesses sufficient Personal authority of the right sort.

Consider Dr. Benjamin Spock, whose Personal authority and special form of Charismatic authority suit him ideally to be a doctor to children; they make him far more fitted for this function than a sharp-tongued, authoritarian taskmaster-type of doctor would be. Dr. Spock *looks* like a baby doctor; he is large and kind and gentle, and he moves gracefully. These qualities, along with his Sapiential authority in medicine, make him a damned good *doctor*. Nevertheless, his thinking and behavior on other matters—in which he has no legitimate claim to Sapiential authority—may often be defective. I would be delighted to have our children in his care, but I am not at all sure that I would be equally pleased to follow all of Dr. Spock's political and other prescriptions for the "good life."

An interesting, and potentially enlightening, problem arises with Aesculapian authority: How does one acquire the skill of behaving in a way that will be perceived as "physicianly"? Why, for example, do some doctors, who have worked hard to obtain their medical credentials, never seem to get the hang of conveying the physician's "gentle, professional manner" to patients? And how have the men who have impersonated doctors so successfully been able to adopt Aesculapian authority convincingly without the necessary preliminaries and to use it so effectively? Questions such as these are open to sociological inquiry, and answers to them should reveal new and unexpected aspects to the nature of the doctor-patient relationship—aspects that could be used in improving it.

The system of authority we are exploring here derived from

Paterson's studies of small groups. Members of a group, he observed, follow certain rules connected with the *function* of the group. Distribution of authority—in its different forms—among members of the group, he noted, allowed for *specialization* and made it possible for the peculiar geniuses of particular group members to be identified and employed for the good of the group. One aim of the group, thus, is to magnify special qualities of group members and, in each case, increase the prospect for their self-fulfillment within the context of the group's formal mission—whether this be to manage a government, to conduct a neighborhood meeting, or to coordinate a particular range of activities in a factory.

OPTIMUM GROUP SIZE

Paterson realized early that group size was an important factor to consider in developing his theory. He began from the first principle that a group should be as large as possible (in order to capitalize on the diversity of individual talents and styles within it) as long as it could continue to function.

The lower limit of stable group size was examined years ago by Georg Simmel, who invented this new version of an old, old saw: "Two's company; three's none." While three (something of a magic number in Western cultures) may be a viable group size in certain circumstances, the history of triumvirates is not reassuring. The foursome seems a good deal more stable. It allows for six different dyads and provides choice without confusion; four thus seems to be the smallest number of persons in a group for the best effect.

The upper limit of stable group size concerns the maximum number of individuals who can carry on meaningful face-to-face interactions in terms of the group's goals and purposes over a period of time. To achieve this, those who interact must know one another well enough to interrelate appropriately. It turns out that a group's effectiveness begins to fall off sharply when the number of members increases beyond ten or twelve.

This estimate of maximum—but not *optimum*—group size tallies rather well with the size of the basic military units (squads, messes), most juries, boards, and cabinets. For example, the Roman legion's basic unit group was six to eight; the toman of the Tatars was ten; the wirgild (mutually responsible group) of the Anglo-Saxons was ten; the Incas' basic social unit was ten; the American Indian war party was ten or eleven; the commando unit was seven to nine; the royal naval messes in the nineteenth century were four to eight; the Communist cell is six to eight; British intelligence has a rule that no more than seven persons should possess most secret information (if more, the probability of a leak increases disproportionately); British cabinets have always held an "inner group" of about eight; the Mafia "family" is also in this range of size.

Why?

It has long been known that man's span of attention is the "magic number" seven, plus or minus two, that is, five to nine. Ordinarily, most people can recall from five to nine digits; some can do much better.

To be an effective member of a group, you have to know something about each of the other members—name, age, sex, status relations with other group members and nongroup members, and so on. You can ordinarily retain five to nine complex aggregations of this sort of personal information. Not having to learn your own data, the *optimum* size of a group, then, would be from five plus one (one = you) to nine plus one, or between six and ten, which, as we have seen, approximates what occurs in practice.

Another approach to the optimum group size involves the use of R. C. Carpenter's formula for expressing group complexity. The number of dyads in a group is $\frac{1}{2}n(n-1)$. Thus, a two-person group has only one dyad; a four-person group has six; a group of eight has twenty-eight. Thus, merely doubling the size of the group from four to eight multiplies the complexity of two-person, face-to-face combinations by 4½. A group of twelve has sixty-six dyadic relations, and one can see that, very soon, the complexity of intragroup relationships becomes too complicated for the human brain to handle.

It can be concluded from this that the president's cabinet, numbering eleven men, is probably too big to work optimally. Efforts by President Nixon to reduce its size in 1971 and by other presidents in earlier years may not have been inspired by wishes to concentrate more "power" in the presidency—as some observers have charged. Rather, the presidents may have wanted to shrink the cabinet because they experienced difficulty in wielding the enormous authority they already had over a cabinet that was unwieldy itself, because it was "unnaturally" overlarge. (Interestingly, one of the world's greatest ideological leaders tried to run a group of thirteen; the group fragmented after a Last Supper.)

FIVE BASIC ROLES

Paterson asked himself what a group would require—in addition to a limitation of its size and a distribution of interwoven authorities—in order to work effectively, and he hit upon the concept of "roles": *the positional embodiment of rules of operation*. Paterson identified just five basic roles:

The Exemplar role: This role is occupied by the person who expresses the *moral feeling* of the group and speaks mainly on matters of *principle*. He is known as a "sound man on the committee." He may not do very much or even say very much, and he is seldom bellicose in his attitudes. He listens a lot, tuning in to the commitment and mood of the group; in this way, he acquires or assumes both Moral and Sapiential authority. He may remain comparatively silent throughout long debates, and then say something like, "I wonder if we don't all feel this way about such-and-such"—and oddly enough, "we" very often *do*. The Exemplar sets the tone of the group and represents the group's moral consensus.

The Exdominus role: The group's Exdominus is the person who concerns himself with the *external relations* between his group and other groups. He is the one who comes to the fore after decisions have been reached and action is to be taken. He tends to be vociferous and sometimes even bellicose. He is often identified as the group's "spokesman." As such, the Exdominus represents his group to the *outside* and has the right to command followers of the consensus of the group; therefore, he possesses Structural authority.

The Indominus (or "concentric") role: The one who occupies this role is concerned with the group's *internal relations*. He acts concentrically, as a *manager of the group*, holding it together against internal strains, "keeping the meeting in order," as a parliamentarian does. He is often known as a "good committeeman" because he knows the ropes of the group, and his application of this knowledge invests him with Structural authority and a particular brand of Sapiential authority.

The Excentric role: For a group to function most effectively, it must receive an input from outside the group—ideas or data that may be disparate or even contrary to the principles of the group. The one who brings in *new information* is the Excentric ("away from the center"). Possession of special knowledge invests him with Sapiential authority. In this role, the Excentric helps move the group toward new or expanded areas of activity. Sometimes he may be regarded as being "out on a limb," but this is tolerated by other group members who recognize the importance of the Excentric's role in advancing the group.

The Mimetic role: This role is assumed by all group members who *follow* the Exemplar, Exdominus, and Indominus. The

Mimetic may be a group member without any specified role other than to participate in the group's activities, or he may be a particular authoritative member of the group. For example, the Exemplar is a Mimetic when he follows the action of the Exdominus; the Exdominus is a Mimetic when the Indominus calls him "out of line" and shuts him up. A Mimetic may also *understudy* one of the other roles, taking it over from the one he is understudying when the circumstances call for it. Being the nucleus of the group, the Mimetics establish the rights of other members to *their* roles and invest them with their appropriate forms of authority.

Paterson's methectics may appear to be a trifle involved, though it contains only four (or six) forms of authority and four (or five) roles in group behavior. One brief example of a group—identifying the authority and role of each member—may snap it all into focus. The war council of the American Indians seems ideally suited for this purpose.

Many Indian war councils—like the war party—had a nucleus of manageable size, usually few more than five men. They were: war chief, peace chief, wise man, shaman, and one or more highly placed subordinates. According to Paterson's system of roles, the peace chief would be the Indominus (or Concentric); the war chief would be the Exdominus; the wise man would be the Exemplar; the shaman (or witch doctor) would be the Excentric; and the subordinates would be the Mimetics. Braves in the war party were Mimetics, too. Overall, this seems to be a sound system; it must have been, for it proved effective over a great many years.

Strange to say, a bureaucracy seems also to be a sound system. It involves the establishment of a range of roles in the form of departments. This gives a certain amount of continuity to the operation of the overall group and eliminates the necessity to think through many different standard forms of information gathering, decision making, and action taking every time the group wants to do something. For all our moans and whines about the horrors of bureaucracies, we seem always to wind up creating more of them. Methectics would seem to explain why.

AUTHORITY AND ROLES FOR EACH
FUNCTIONAL TYPE

Before considering how Typology and methectics can be combined into a system for suitably organizing human beings in ways that serve both the uniqueness and the diversity of humanity, it may be useful to explore some of the mechanics and effects of combining the two concepts into typo-methectics.

Nowhere in human affairs does it seem that methectics and Typology merge more closely and with greater effect than in the process of gathering information, drawing conclusions from it, basing decisions upon those conclusions, and taking actions on those decisions—in short, the functions of human beings participating in group activities. The full range of those functions involves the social contributions of persons of different types, exerting the different forms of authority. Often, blocks or short circuits in the process result in serious errors of omission or commission. On many occasions the ideal process must give way to something less than ideal.

It appears, for example, that conclusions surrounding the atomic bombing of a Japanese city were presented in so slovenly a way that decisions were reached in which little or no attention was paid to the human, social, and political consequences in either the short or the long range. Certain other courses of action, which properly might have been explored, did not receive adequate attention. The result—with which we are still living—was something that may have been *unnecessarily* less than ideal.

A particular man exercising authority of one sort or another colors that authority by his personal style—his *Typological* characteristics. Understanding his Typology makes it possible to see ways in which his special characteristics can best serve his position of authority and the goals of the group. It also becomes possible to predict whether he will need special help and encouragement in some aspects of the study-conclusion-decision-action process. For instance, his Typology may indicate a tendency to want to "telescope" the process; President Johnson was inclined in this direction, as Mrs. Johnson indicated when she said, "Lyndon wants to do everything *now*." Or knowledge of a particular authority's Typology may suggest that he tends to let the process run on, not reaching the usable conclusions from which decision making and action derive; something like this might be expected from someone of Eugene McCarthy's Typology.

The existence of "styles" of management is widely recognized. Until now, however, there has been no way of using our knowledge of personal management styles (in any but the most general way) to *optimize* both their effectiveness and the effectiveness of the group enterprises in which they are applied. Combining Typology and methectics into the system of typo-methectics seems to provide a way of overcoming this obstacle to the fulfillment of the individual, the group he serves, and the larger realm that is served by the group.

A good way of looking at this is to consider what forms of methectic authority and roles are best suited for each of the typological functions.

THINKING

For example, all other things (e.g., intelligence and experience) being equal, the Thinking-type of person will most easily and appropriately exercise Sapiential authority. The Thinking person is continuous, is likely to possess both knowledge and a theory with which to give well-organized *authoritative* advice on matters, and is *not* likely to come up with totally haywire schemes for the group to act upon. Such an individual is likely also to assume Structural authority in the role of either Indominus or Exdominus, or sometimes even as the Excentric. And, on occasion, the person may assume two different roles with two different forms of authority, though usually not simultaneously.

T. T. Paterson, for example, was elected head of the professional committee at the University of Strathclyde and served, therefore, as the Indominus with Structural authority. This severely limited the application of his expert knowledge on fields of concern to the committee, for his proper function in that role was to maintain the internal integrity of the committee and to keep business flowing—not to expound on new ideas or background information. That would be the function of the Excentric, exercising Sapiential authority. Paterson's way around this obstacle was to request occasionally to be allowed by the committee to stand down from the chair and have another professor conduct the meeting, while Paterson himself would introduce information on behalf of his department for the committee to consider. Without making this shift in roles, Paterson could have been seen as using the chair to bias his own argument, or else he would have deprived the committee of his valuable knowledge and experience. Sometimes, you *can* have it both ways—if you know how.

Another instance in which Paterson found it necessary to keep the authorities he possessed separate from each other involved his relations with white South Africans. In counseling them to abandon apartheid on *administrative grounds*, he exercised his Sapiential authority as an expert in management. He never asserted Moral authority on this matter by scolding them for being immoral people because of the way they treated the black African. No people with a set of customs and traditions wants to hear that they are immoral (not even the Germans of World War II). They are willing, however, to listen seriously to advice on matters that may have a moral component if the matters are discussed from an "operational" point of view. Paterson suggested to the South Africans that they should improve the workings of their industry and civil service by continuously upgrading the jobs that could legally be held by black Africans, who otherwise could take jobs of manual labor only. Since Paterson's counsel, a whole new type of job classification has appeared in the South African Republic—"manual labor" that does not involve the use of hands.

These two examples, in the context of typo-methectics, may help explain why Plato's pursuit of the philosopher-king ideal failed and probably was doomed to failure. According to typo-methectics, an individual may assume but one role at a time, preferably one suited to the authority he possesses and to his Typology. One would be hard-pressed, indeed, to draw up the typo-methectic specifications for a philosopher-king that might be met by a single human being: Plato could not do it, in theory or practice.

FEELING

The *Feeling*-type of person is obviously going to gravitate toward the Exemplar's role, asserting his Moral authority in composing and then communicating a picture of the group's principles. Because these individuals are on the side of the angels—insofar as the objectives of the enterprise are concerned—they sometimes assume Structural authority in addition to their Moral authority. This can be dangerous—even with very good Moral authorities like President Eisenhower. The combination of Structural and massive Moral authorities is the stuff that dictators are made of. It was probably a wise move for the English to reject Churchill as prime minister following his many wartime triumphs. It would not do for a man of such immense political power and personal and Moral authority to be running the country during what was foreseen as an extremely difficult postwar period. Nor does it seem a coincidence that the Chinese have done their utmost to retain Mao while at the same time preventing him from exercising total top authority. To a man like Mao, Structural authority that is carried by the position of head of state is simply not enough. Such men believe that their great vision, feeling, and moral infallibility should be put into effect in every conceivable way, and human affairs are not up to that sort of thing. People require planning, agreement, know-how, technical ability, and many other things that the great moral megatypes usually underestimate in favor of their high regard for their own superior views of things.

Aside from the threat that a person with strong Moral authority presents in taking over an enterprise and heading it for disaster, there is a risk also in having too many persons exercising Moral authority. A group composed entirely of Exemplars probably wouldn't accomplish anything, except perhaps to decide how everyone *felt* about things.

One should be careful, also, to ensure that it is the feeling and morality of the group that the Exemplar reflects and not his own. Whether done deliberately or completely unconsciously and innocently, the Exemplar's imposing his own feelings upon the group—instead of sensing and expressing the climate of the group's feeling—can be gravely misleading. (Of course, it may be that the Exemplar's and the group's feelings are identical; this frequently happens by virtue of the Exemplar's strong Feeling function, which facilitates his "resonating" with the mood of the group.)

A minor but engaging example of a Feeling-type's coloring his rendition of another's feelings with his own occurred in a television production on William Blake, artist, poet, mystic, and probably Intuitive-Feeling-type. His interpreter was the Feeling-Intuitive poet Allen Ginsberg.

Ginsberg's view was that the authentic voice of Blake was that of the "ancient days," echoing past miseries and reflecting gravely on present ones. That voice *was* present in Blake, but his most clarion tones rang of prophecy, with revealing visions of many futures—some beautiful, some terrifying. Blake's revelations and visions of the *future*—laced with profound compassion, sorrow, joy, hope, and fears—played very little part in Ginsberg's portrait of the artist. Ginsberg's performance was interesting, skillful, and sincere. However, there is little doubt that Ginsberg's Blake was Ginsberg's and not Blake's Blake.

Oddly, Ginsberg's apparent error in interpreting Blake did not prevent the program from being very enjoyable, for he has a deep poetic feeling for Blake, which he communicated movingly. Nevertheless, it would appear that his understanding of and feeling for Blake would be enhanced, broadened, and deepened if he were able to recognize not only the similarities in his own and Blake's view of the cosmos (they do, after all, share leading typological functions) but the differences as well. The huge strength and penetrating quality of Blake's vision is shown by his ability to burn bright in the souls of those far removed from him in space, time, and temperament. His poems have a universality that makes them appeal to those of differing temperaments, and their impact seems to increase with familiarity; they are antientropic.

Ginsberg might have done well, before trying to reflect Blake's feeling, to reflect on these lines of the man considered by some to have been one of the greatest poets who ever lived:

> The Vision of Christ that thou dost see
> Is my Vision's Greatest Enemy.
> Thine has a great hook nose like thine,
> Mine has a snub nose like to mine.
> Thine is a friend of All Mankind
> Mine speaks in parables to the Blind.
> Thine loves the same world that mine hates,
> Thy Heaven doors are my Hell gates. . . .
>
> . . . . .
>
> Both read the Bible day and night,
> But thou read'st black where I read white.

SENSATION

What is required of a group's Exdominus—and often of the Indominus as well—is *action*, and none of the four typological functions fills that particular bill as well as the *Sensation*-type. His abilities at solving problems—internal to the group or external to the enterprise—endow this person with Personal authority that he uses to "get things done." The discontinuity of this type often makes for fits and starts and rapid shifts from one problem or project to another. The Sensation-type sometimes assumes Structural authority, but this can be less than desirable in cases in which foresight—which the Sensation-type lacks—is required; this type may be brilliant on the tactical level but utterly incapable of strategy.

INTUITIVE

Although the Thinking-type can fulfill the duties of the Excentric adequately, the one best suited to this role—better suited than he is to any other role—is the *Intuitive*. The person with a strong Intuition function is constantly in pursuit of that which is just beyond the horizon of the attainable; in the role of the Excentric, he can bring the group's attention to information and *potential* possibilities that the Thinking-type would never dream of suggesting. The Intuitive thus asserts Sapiential, Personal, and probably Charismatic authority. His charisma, if he possesses any, may put him into the position of Structural authority; this can be disappointing because the enterprise is not likely to move forward under a leader who is swinging on a star, as it were. Clearly, in the competition over Structural authority the Thinking-type wins hands down.

While it would in most cases be wisest, then, to select a Thinking-type as top authority, it should be remembered that he is unlikely to be very responsive to people's feelings (Feeling being his weakest function). He may simply ignore the feelings of the group and of those to whom the group must relate. Or, he may recognize the value of considering people's feelings, but, lacking the capacity to do this as well as others can, may operate under totally mistaken notions of the way people feel. Here is where a Feeling-type with supportive, Moral authority in the role of Exemplar can often save the day.

Also, the Thinking-type with Structural authority may be able to generate a well-organized plan for a group but be deficient in finding effective ways of putting it into action for optimal effect. This is where the Sensation-type can serve so well as the Exdominus—communicating his personal authority to groups and agencies with which his enterprise must deal.

10

Using Typo-Methectics
for Group Effectiveness

It would appear, from this brief presentation of the mechanics of typo-methectics and from practical applications of the theory in real organizational and management problems, that it is an effective instrument for producing abstractions concerning the humane management of mankind. It was once said that it is better to remain a poor fisherman than to meddle with the governing of men. This may no longer be so. It appears possible now to handle, in a systematic way, complicated relationships between people who have a wide range of different points of view and who must function in different roles with various interrelated forms of authority. With typo-methectics, we can organize enterprises of all kinds and dimensions, achieving in each case an effectively balanced diversity of human qualities.

Typo-methectics can thus be used to select and organize persons for the most effective pursuit of a particular goal. It can also be used to analyze existing enterprises to see what is good about them, what is bad about them, and how to make them work most effectively. One key is to maintain an approximate mix of types, roles, and authorities.

An Ideal Group

A stereotypic, idealized group would be composed in the following manner for optimum effectiveness. The leader would probably be a Thinking-type, possessing Structural authority, of course, plus Sapiential and perhaps Personal authority. He would assume the role of Indominus and, on occasion, the Exdominus role when converting the group's decision into action or communicating with those external to the group. He would be supported—and checked—by a Feeling-type in the Exemplar role, possessing Moral authority (perhaps spiked with Personal or even Charismatic authority). A Sensation-type would assume the Exdominus role (when the leader was not occupying it, say, in "formal appearances") and act also as a Mimetic to the leader's Indominus role; he would possess Personal and Sapiential authority, at least. The Excentric role would best be taken by an Intuitive-type with Sapiential and Personal—preferably, Charismatic—authority. Mimetics would complete the group with a distribution of types and authorities fitting the roles they would understudy and the requirements for their effective support of the group's activities.

Achieving precisely that mix is not absolutely necessary for a group to function; performance will drop off, however, as the range of diversity and suitable matching of type, authority, and role diminish.

Consider, for example, a system with a very limited range of diversity in its components: the dictatorship. With authority concentrated in one person, the system has almost no flexibility and very little range of potential expression. *Biologically*, such a system is unsound, which is why a dictatorship is a dud system.

Mao Tse-tung is unquestionably correct when he says that the responsibility for making a group (nation) work effectively lies not with a single ruler (as with Mao himself) but with *human-*

ity. The trouble is that "humanity" must operate within the limits of the human brain. We are not, after all, termites; being highly complex, cerebrate animals, possessing a great diversity of modes of expression, does not make it easy for "rule by humanity" to be achieved by our brain.

Almost as unworkable as humanity's ruling itself through the dictates of individuals is the notion, being expressed more and more today, that a key to the "governability" of the human being ought to be sought if we want to establish utopia—or at least, if mankind is going to avoid catastrophe by man's own hand. Both of these views appear to be the wrong way around.

What *should* be sought, it seems, is *a way to produce a government that is suitable for human beings*, not a concept of the "ideal" government. No nation now has a "humane government." It should be obvious, also, that discovery of a system for creating a government for governing people humanely would immediately indicate: (1) what is wrong with structure and function—the *character*—of small systems (smaller than governments) in their management and optimization of human uniqueness and diversity; and (2) what can be done to modify these smaller systems—business, social, political, professional, even familial—so that they will work more fruitfully for people.

It is important to emphasize that all of this is not to suggest that the world's great governmental systems—particularly the marvelous Anglo-American ones—should be spurned. Compared with systems that have already sprung from man's imagination, however, one must conclude that today's reality is substantially substandard. At best, we seem to be rushing headlong into a third-rate "brave new world," largely because we behave so sluggishly and slovenly when it comes to the important matters of human relations and the role of the mind in society.

It may be that politics and government are—in the strictest sense of the word—*incomprehensible* without typo-methectics or some other form of systematic, theoretical framework for study and discussion. Incomprehensible or not, the *practice* of politics and government in one form or another has been "enjoyed" by people for many centuries. Lacking a systematic theory and language with which to relate human nature and the business of governing, human beings have striven in many ways and on various levels of government and politics to achieve a workable human mixture of leadership and authority. People seem to "know," in some mysterious and obscure way, roughly what a workable human mixture is. They do not know, however, *what* it is that they know—for this has never been formally stated—or *why* they know it. Humans just seem to sense—as a wolf pack does—that they need a stable leadership to govern them, a leadership that is flexible enough to survive without, at the same time, being so flexible and unpredictable as to make life impossible.

All of this suggests strongly that a kind of typo-methectics "instinct" may actually be deeply ingrained—or "engrammed" —into man's very nature. Whether or not human beings, indeed, have natural instincts for the requirements of government and politics, it is clear that they must have a way of enabling free and willing participation in the business of governing; otherwise, chaos would threaten the survival of the species. Merely having goals for a government to pursue in the interests of the society it governs is not enough; there must also be some institutionalized *system* for doing such things as handling disagreements on matters of policy.

A MISTAKE OF MARX AND ENGELS

Marx and Engels, in believing that communism would "inevitably" follow capitalism, presumably overlooked the necessity for building a supportive bureaucratic superstructure under top leadership. They supposed that all the necessary skills for operating the new community government would be provided by the many highly trained persons emerging from the wreckage of capitalism. In the communist view, only minor administrative assistance would have to be supplied while the remains of the capitalist state withered. However, communism did not start where Marx and Engels predicted it would—on the ruins of capitalism. The capitalistic state did not crumble and wither and leave behind the machinery of government, ready-made, to be administered by the proletarian managers. Because Marx and Engels ignored the necessity for constructing an administrative superstructure that would be suitable for governing people, *two* great communist powers emerged, both deplorably deficient in modern administrative skills, both lacking any but the most rudimentary form of democratic traditions for governing humanely. Furthermore, these two great communist states are bitterly opposed to each other, something which Marx and Engels, in their innocence, would have deemed impossible.

RICHARD M. NIXON AS LEADER

The need for "something more" in assuming top leadership was certainly true in the case of Richard M. Nixon in 1969, when he added the Charismatic authority of the office of the president to his already considerable Sapiential authority as a quondam vice-president, to his Structural authority of *being* the president, and to his own consummate political skill for wielding those authorities. Something *was* missing, and the American public knew it but had no language with which to express this knowledge. It didn't do simply to say that the effects of Mr. N.'s personal style were divisive instead of bringing the country together. Nor did it pay to complain that the president was not very inspiring—it was well known that vision and charisma are not in the man's nature. Those were mere matters of fact about the man who was—as LBJ once responded to criticism about himself—"the only president you've got." It was, therefore, necessary to look elsewhere for a "something . . . missing" in the Nixon leadership about which something constructive could be done.

With typo-methectics, it should be possible to *diagnose* in precise terminology what is ailing or missing in a top authority, to *prognose* the probable course and outcome of the ailment, and, with hope, to *prescribe* regimens for correcting the ailment or lessening its effects on the body politic—capitalizing at every turn on the leader's strong points. This is closely analogous to a supportive therapeutic approach to effective medical management of patients, which has proved its effectiveness over many thousands of man-years of practical application.

The theory also makes it clear that under the *best* conditions you do not get something for nothing. For example, if you want to choose a Lincoln for your leader, you must take him "warts and all." You will benefit from his charisma, knowledge, humanity, and vision. But you will be dealing with a man who can be very difficult when it comes to matters of ordinary methodology. He will complicate things by insisting upon being totally accessible to all input—people, information, and so on. If you choose a Nixon—typologically, Sensation-Thinking to Lincoln's Intuitive-Feeling—you will have a different problem altogether. You will benefit by the talents of a master politician and a legal mind that can grapple quickly and effectively with difficult problems that would have many other equally intelligent men on the ropes before the fight began. You won't mind too much that he isn't "cuddly"; you will understand that he prefers a little distance and likes to do his grappling with problems alone. But you mustn't reproach him for lacking charisma; while he does not possess this indefinable quality, the office he occupies *does*, and this is probably more than enough for the job. Also, you mustn't despair that Mr. N. does not appear able to work up any inspiring vision to "move the people," because that's not his bag, either.

Should your choice of a leader be a Jack Kennedy, you may have your appetite for charisma and vision satisfied, but you should not expect much warmth from a detached and cool Thinking-Intuitive-type who would prefer to have people like him but doesn't mind terribly if they do not. The same could not be said if your choice of leader were an LBJ, an immensely capable Sensation and Feeling combination who moaned a lot of the time about not being well liked by the people (until an old friend confided to him that maybe it was because he might not be a terribly likable man). And so on.

Predictability and Evaluation of Leaders' Performances

The important point to all of this is that the qualities of the leaders just discussed are not only consistent with their typologies but *could have been predicted.* In addition, each man's typological characteristics could be combined with his professional qualifications for evaluation methectically to *estimate* the kind and quality of performance that might be expected from him in various capacities as, say, lawyer, congressman, senator, committee chairman, vice-president, and president. This sort of analysis could, therefore, make possible the identification and optimal support of the individual's strengths and the provision of special help when and where he needs it. Thus, even failure can be anticipated.

Vitalness of a Leader's Morale-Building Capability

If there is one skill without which a new leader's failure is assured, it is the capacity to assess, raise, rebuild, and foster *morale.* As Napoleon said, morale is to the physical as ten is to one.

There are no simple formulas for morale building. People of many different typologies have achieved it in many different ways. Nevertheless, it is enormously important to the enterprise that the leader recognize and clearly understand the preeminence of heeding the quality of the morale of the organization. It would seem at least prudent to inquire carefully into a potential leader's understanding of morale problems and his capacity for dealing with them effectively.

This rule applies equally in successful enterprises and in ones that are faltering. High morale in a healthy organization may be made higher still by a leader who can come up with challenging new possibilities; the leader must suggest them with tact and good sense, however, by presenting his plans for progress *within the morality of the organization.* If he doesn't know what that is, he can inquire from the Feeling-types who exercise the Moral authority of the Exemplars in the organization. They can usually be recognized by their cogitative and deliberately thoughtful appearance and slow verbal delivery in staff conferences.

The Leader's Use of Typo-Methectics

The new leader then must introduce his new plans for the organization in a nonthreatening, reassuring manner, such as: "From the splendid history of success that this organization boasts, the goals that I am setting will, I am sure, interest and intrigue you. With a less experienced and capable group, I would hardly dare mention them." In saying that, the leader would be showing a "better still" face. He would clearly *not* be questioning the organization's previous high performance; doing so would probably evoke anger and hostility in an organization whose good record was well established and morale was already high.

As mentioned, the leader who is knowledgeable about typo-methectics will pay special attention to the Exemplary members of the organization. Through them he can communicate that he sees them as members of a successful group of which he can rightfully demand new exertions, while at no time will it be implied that the organization's earlier efforts were not admirable. If he does this honestly and convincingly, he can be sure that the Exemplars will convey to the rest of the group his appreciation of the organization's fine qualities and his future plans for it.

All of this can be a tricky enough business in a healthy organization. In an ailing one in which morale is poor and the members are, at best, dispirited and, at worst, cynical or even openly disaffected, it is even trickier. The new leader is likely—without knowledge of methectics—to believe that a simple and direct approach will straighten everything out. Actual cases in which enterprises were failing and morale plummeting do not support this view. Attending first to morale may seem like an indirect attack on the problem, but it is often the best approach, even under the worst circumstances.

In 1917, for example, after the disastrous Nivelle offensive in April, the French army mutinied on a massive scale. At times, it looked as if a complete collapse and revolution might occur. Henri Philippe Pétain took over. He shot a few—a very few—mutineers; this was, after all, near the end of one of the bloodiest wars in French history. Yet he became *respected, remembered,* and *revered* for rebuilding the shattered French armies. He did this by first seeing that his soldiers got better food, drink, shelter, and rest. In addition, he greatly curtailed adventurous offensive operations; those he did undertake were limited and frequently successful with little loss of life. He could not undo the appalling slaughter that the French fighting forces had absorbed in earlier years. He did rebuild the morale of the survivors sufficiently, however, for the French armies to prevail at a time when their survival was very much in doubt. His soldiers rewarded him with their devotion and the nickname "Papa Pétain."

Because morale is so important to an organization's future, it would be prudent for a new leader to devise ways of determining whether the morale of the enterprise he takes over is high or low. This may, in fact, be *the* crucial question upon which the future of the leader's rule will depend. Any planning he does to raise morale need not interfere with the more general, overall, long-range planning for the enterprise but can become part of it. In any case, morale must be given particular attention, whether the enterprise is healthy or failing.

One who takes over an organization-in-being is likely either to be awed by its tradition of success—if it *is* successful—or to be intimidated or challenged by its history of failure. Being awed at success often inhibits changes that can be made easily and beneficially by a new leader and would be welcomed. It is easy for a new leader to discover things that most members of the organization have wanted done and to do them, if he agrees that they would be beneficial. But he should indicate that his action is merely an extension of the organization's usual way of doing things. Moreover, he should make it clear that his aim is for the organization to "do even better," never for a moment suggesting that things were not as good as they might have been. By stating his aim to "do even better" than the organization had done before, the new leader seems immediately to become part of the tradition and morality of the organization—to be a component of the continuity of the department, firm, state, nation, or whatever.

In an ailing organization, the "new-broom" technique is often used. The new manager dashes in with much imbroglio and announces that reform must be instantaneous, everybody must change for the better or it will be the worse for them, and so on. In actuality, the technique is usually the worse for the enterprise, because morale is assaulted. (Sometimes, this approach is taken by a leader who has been in power for a long while in a failing organization and is desperate to retain his command. The results are usually no better than they are for the *new* leader who tries to sweep the slate clean.)

The new-broom approach is a favorite scenario of revolutions of all sorts—from the right *or* the left. Mussolini was said to have given Italy back its self-respect by making the trains run on time. Wedded as he was to melodrama, Mussolini could not see that short-term gains usually end in disaster if they are not wedded to the continuity of the enterprise.

Although an organization may be dilapidated and demoralized, it does not necessarily lack achievement, able members, and at least a spark of potential for succeeding. Identifying those survival factors requires application of the "military method" that generals such as Pétain, Haig, Montgomery, Alexander, Rommel, and MacArthur used in rebuilding the morale of routed forces. This method consists of acquiring quickly, from a variety of sources within the organization, two kinds of information about the enterprise: assets and liabilities. Obvious? Certainly. Yet, how often is this simple procedure actually applied? Rarely, very rarely.

Whatever the leader's plans and projects, they must thereafter be put forward in terms of known assets and liabilities. Just as any institution, at its best, has its liabilities, none is likely, even at its very worst, to lack assets altogether. At the Spithead Mutiny of 1797, Admiral "Black Dick" Howe assessed the British sailors' chief assets as their profound patriotism and dedication to defending their country against the French. With astounding diplomatic skill, the admiral treated the mutineers as erring *patriots*—and resolved the mutiny bloodlessly. Similarly, Pétain knew his soldiers had been ill done by in the fatuous Nivelle offensive. The marshal asserted his Structural authority swiftly, but even more vigorously applied his Moral authority by caring for the stricken armies' personal needs.

To perceive assets in a faltering organization, and liabilities in a succeeding one, often requires sympathy, intelligence, and imagination. Sometimes, it also requires a refusal to be put off by those who suppose themselves to be knowledgeable. A top manager must be able and willing to examine and evaluate with some detachment his *human resources*, as well as the physical and other ones, before launching ambitious new programs. Old techniques, such as the military method of assessing liabilities and assets, combined with an overall management theory such as typo-methectics, should make this difficult business of governing a good deal less risky than it would be without such useful instruments.

Typo-Methectics for Nonutopian, Rational Government

It may seem an extravagant claim (but perhaps only because it is a unique one) that the theory of typo-methectics provides the beginnings of a practical way, for the first time, to produce nonutopian, rational government (in the generic sense of the word "government").

So far, every rational government has been utopian because it has presumed one of two conditions. One is that the governed will govern themselves (which is hopelessly improbable *without* a system for doing it and a terrifying probability *with* such a system). The other utopian presumption is that a psychosocial "mutation" of some sort in humanity will make mankind suddenly very different—peaceful, loving, unselfish, wise, and manageable. The latter would be nice, of course, but it would hardly be prudent to count on its occurring.

Not only is the human species unlikely to experience a "great mutation" that would make humanity more manageable, but we had all better hope that this sort of sudden change *doesn't* come about: things would be much more likely to alter for the worse than for the better. The overwhelming majority of biological mutations in living things are lethal, and there is no reason to expect that the consequences of great and rapid transformation in the biosocial sphere would be any less grave.

11

Application of
Typo-Methectics to
Particular Situations

The Cult of Personality in the Soviet Union

The impressive Aleksei Kosygin, in an interview with reporters for *Life*, emphasized clearly and repeatedly that the Soviet leadership was collective and did not depend upon the "cult of personality." Mr. Kosygin bears this out personally, for he is clearly an intelligent, rational Thinking-type whose arguments were oddly referred to by *Life* as "chilling." In fact, they are neither chilling nor warming, nor were they intended to be such. They were derived from principles that Mr. Kosygin considers to be based on sound premises. There was no threatening and no wheedling. Mr. Kosygin stated clearly enough that the Russians did not intend to desert North Vietnam, and he asked the same question that many Americans have asked, "What are *you* doing in Vietnam at all?"

Mr. Kosygin spoke with authority, and clearly he has *great* authority, but that was not what came across in this talk. It is clear that his is no dazzling personality. Neither did he give the feeling that was communicated by Stalin—sinister power held in reserve. He was not manipulative. He did not appeal to love and friendship; he did not threaten hatred. He simply stated his views as a competent doctor or engineer might state them. He was using almost undiluted Sapiential authority without much humor or wit, and it seems that this is what "chilled" his American interlocutors. This is a political style that is not seen frequently in the United States—perhaps the only recent exponent of it was former Senator Eugene McCarthy, who became an editor at a book-publishing company in Manhattan.

It seems that the Russians mean something fairly explicit when they claim to have eliminated the cult of personality. Their last three leaders—Lenin, Stalin, Khrushchev—were men who, for very different reasons and in entirely different ways, exercised, along with their Structural authority, great Personal authority.

With Lenin, this derived from his sapience. As a young man he was referred to as "Starik" (the old one) because of his inspiring nature and the belief that he was a moral man. He used this Personal authority little, did not manipulate people, and disliked fulsome references to himself.

Stalin was a very different sort of animal. He gained great eminence almost entirely by manipulation. Having achieved the peak of Structural authority, he attempted to acquire Moral, Sapiential, and Charismatic authorities. It appears that in spite of his most vigorous attempts—which included mass murder, large-scale forgery, and indecent indulgence in self-promotion—Stalin did not quite succeed. Indeed, once the Russians were sure that he was dead, they did their best to repudiate him.

Nevertheless, the Russian people were still dominated by a man whose Personal authority was considerable: Khrushchev. After his fall, the style of government changed. Why did the new and more admirable Soviet government seem to chill *Life's* observers?

The stereotype for an American politician is clearly an Extraverted Sensation and Thinking combination. Many politicians are not naturally of this ilk, but all have to make a show of being so because it is the American cultural ideotype. That such a persona is considered essential by the electorate tells us much about the political system and much about the United States. Some other countries might find our preferred political characteristics objectionable because their cultural ideotypes are different.

Whatever the Russian stereotype for a politician is, there is no reason to suppose that it is the same as the American. Indeed, it is probably very different. The stereotypic Russian (and this does not mean that any more Russians naturally meet this stereotype than Americans naturally meet theirs) probably has an enlarged sense of the past and the future but is only modestly concerned with the present. Thus Russians appear as concerned primarily with Feeling and Intuition. They seem to be not particularly adept at manipulation and to be liable to be manipulated by those who are.

The history of Russia supports this. That huge country has moved forward by a series of jerky convulsions which outsiders have often thought would ruin it completely. Doubtless any smaller country would have been ruined. It seems that, so far, Russia has found no adequate way of harnessing and directing the energy of its Sensation-types, who are hardly suited for furthering distant prospects in a future that means little or nothing to them. Indeed, they can be extraordinarily dangerous in such projects. (Stalin, to further his interpretation of Lenin's blueprint of the future, murdered millions of Russians, apparently unaware that such brutal actions might change the nature of what was sought for the future.) Any questioning of the nature of present actions, however dubious they might be, has been generally treated as ruinous to the golden future. Sensation-types have a highly concrete future; when they entertain the idea of the future, it must be in a highly concrete form.

The United States has found a proper activity for Sensation-types: obtaining wealth and, in this way, authority. However, this too creates problems; modern societies, like modern businesses, are becoming far more complex, and other types are not merely needed but essential. The manipulativeness of Sensation-types is necessary for survival, yet too much of a good thing at the wrong time and in the wrong place can endanger survival.

For somewhat different reasons, in recent years neither the Americans nor the Russians have been willing, generally, to recognize that there may be inherent differences among men. Although their actions have not always been consistent with the view that one man is as good as another, this has been more or less the American view, from President Andrew Jackson on, a view that the Russians paralleled in Lysenkoism. However, Americans have cherished their Sensation-types (who most exemplify the notion of the wholly adaptable man), while Russians have been extremely ambivalent toward them, at best. Worst of all, the valuable task of moneymaking has been made immoral and difficult in the Soviet Union. Contrary to Ayn Rand's view, this was done on principle by Thinking-types more powerful than she, working from different premises.

The collective leadership and the attempt to eradicate the cult of personality seem to be a Russian substitute for the infinitely complex system of checks and balances in the United States. The aim is to further continuity and rationality; it is a matter of debate whether it is likely to succeed. Russia seems to have been faced by problems deriving from a cultural ideotype that has a relatively small place for the present and substantial places for the past and future. This can hardly be due only to Russian social organization, although some selection seems to have worked against Sensation-types—they crop up in Russian history in truly monstrous forms: Peter the Great, Rasputin,

Malinovsky, and Stalin come to mind. It seems unfortunate that the social controls in Russia have never allowed these admirable qualities to be harnessed for the general good.

Chinese Politics

ROLE OF A CONTINUOUS MAN OF PRINCIPLE, CHOU EN-LAI

Chou En-lai is an astoundingly durable political animal. We have further evidence of the esteem with which he is held by both friends and enemies. That the high-principled statesman is much valued in China is very evident from such books as Maurice Collis's *Foreign Mud* and Dennis Bloodworth's *The Chinese Looking-Glass*. In Collis's book, the Chinese appear as always keen to teach the "barbarian dogs," as they described the British, how to behave virtuously.

Chou is probably a Thinking-Intuitive whose great Sapiential authority matches Chairman Mao's vast Moral and Charismatic authorities. Because he is more detached than Mao and has much greater foresight of an organized kind, Chou's presence is vital for reducing the impact of Mao's outbursts of moral inspiration, picking up the bits afterward, and getting people to keep on the job. People do not revere him as they do Mao; but as the decades have passed, Chou has become recognized, both at home and abroad, as an indispensable man. His integrity as a devoted Chinese Communist has become something more generalized, and his word, even when what he says is not especially palatable, is trusted.

Countries and political parties are unlikely to flourish unless they have their quota of men like Chou En-lai. Such men can be driven from politics in a variety of ways. Chou probably resembles the late Adlai Stevenson as much as he resembles anyone in the West. Stevenson's capacity for ironical detachment probably did him a good deal of harm in the rollicking days of the New Frontiersmen. By good luck or good judgment, China seems quite happy about Chou's detachment. Indeed, detachment is considered a virtue toward which even the expansive Mao aspires. What in one country would be considered a shortcoming may be seen elsewhere as a virtue. This virtue has been enhanced by Chou's longevity, durability, and consistency over the years. He is not a poet-warrior-emperor like Mao, but a great mandarin-administrator-conciliator who keeps in mind the long-term goals and the principles of his political stance. This partnership between Mao and Chou extending over forty years is worth the most careful typo-methectic inquiry.

THE CULTURAL REVOLUTION AND CHAIRMAN MAO

Why should an aging revolutionary like Mao quite deliberately gamble the safety of his huge country on the "cultural revolution," a scheme that looks to most outsiders like a desperate fling? Mao himself is reported to have been taken by surprise by the unexpectedly violent results of "just a few posters."

It seems clear enough that Mao precipitated the Cultural Revolution because he was concerned with the growing grip of a politico-managerial bureaucracy, which he felt was destroying the spirit of the Long March. He saw with abhorrence a hierarchical society displacing the China of his heart and imagination.

Everywhere in a film on China telecast by the BBC in 1971, there was emphasis on the great importance of practice as opposed to theory. Unless I'm much mistaken, this is a traditional Chinese approach, for the Chinese have long been famous for their pragmatism. They have been as untheoretical in science as in war and in religion. Mao was asserting the primacy of traditional Chinese values combined with his own particular dislike of "specialists," which, since he is a generalist, is very understandable.

To the eye of the Western commentator, it appears that the Cultural Revolution deteriorated into near-anarchy and has petered out. Mao seems too old for another fling of this kind.

The question remains: What exactly was he attempting? Of course, it would offend him to have his deeply felt vision subjected to anything so useless and impractical as *theory*, but luckily there isn't much that he can do about it. A warrior-poet-folk leader like Mao is unlikely to see much virtue in the plans and schemes of the Thinking theoreticians and the Sensation social manipulators; their activities fill him with suspicious concern. What had evidently happened over the years, as he perceived it, was that the sense of unity that reached its apogee in the legendary Long March was being replaced by something wholly different. As a Feeling-Intuitive man—a moral visionary —Mao believes, rightly or wrongly, that he more than anyone else resonates to the deepest feelings of his fellow Chinese. Foresight is not his strongest card; although his imagination is powerful and he is highly intelligent, he tends to go forward while looking, so to speak, in a rear-view mirror to Chinese history and, above all, to the most richly emotive period of his own life: the Long March.

In an ancient country like China, which has been ruled by a great bureaucracy for millennia, Mao is absolutely correct in his belief that oppression by abstracting and manipulating bureaucrats who become increasingly out of touch with people's needs and feelings represents a grave and omnipresent danger. His aim or goal, which is to ensure that the Chinese bureaucracy does not strangle his new China, seems wholly admirable. The question the BBC asked was whether the means he used were likely to attain such a goal. Perhaps understandably, without a theory like typo-methectics, the BBC was unable to deal with the even more pressing question: What can we learn from this? Yet, there is a great deal for all countries in the world to learn from Mao's experience.

It seems likely that, as in the Great Leap Forward, Chairman Mao made the grave, gross (but, in view of his Typology, very predictable) error of confusing whatever Structural authority he possessed—and still possesses as chairman of the Chinese Communist party and government—with his gigantic Moral, Charismatic, Personal, and Sapiential authorities. It was his Sapiential authority that became seriously questioned after the fiasco of the Great Leap Forward. According to Mao's own account, the planners and bureaucrats then did their best to keep him away from administrative, technical, and economic matters. In view of the disaster they had suffered in consequence of Mao's moral vision, one can see their point.

There is no evidence that anyone challenged Mao's Moral authority and visionary status; certain leaders merely felt that he did not understand the nature and needs of a modern technological society. From about 1959 to 1966 they apparently managed to keep Mao more or less insulated from the decision making process—much to his vexation. They succeeded in using the bureaucratic machinery—which he so despises—to his disadvantage. What they had not reckoned with was Mao's capacity to employ his other authorities to evade their vigilance. To them he was an extinct volcano but, as volcanologists know, such a volcano may be cooking up a vast eruption like Krakatau or Mont Pelée.

Since neither Mao nor his technologist-bureaucratic opponents had an adequate theory of human relationships and administrative change, they were all forced to use the lingo of Chinese Marxism. Consequently, it became difficult for outsiders to follow the twists and turns of events. Mao employed his enormous Moral and Charismatic authorities to force through his new moral vision of a "pure" revolutionary society that would be eternally cleansed by what he considered a functional equivalent of the Long March. To achieve this, he unleashed the Red Guards. Mao's feelings about the Cultural Revolution were that it resembled in some way the Long March, the great romantic episode of his legend-making life. What he had not taken into account was that the context of the march was thirty years—but for an expansive FN man, what is thirty years? When the FN man is Chinese, moreover, it is little more than a change of seasons.

For the young people of the Red Guards, however, it was something very different. They had been ordered, coordinated, driven, trained, constrained for years, and now the godlike Mao was unleashing them as a salvationary purge for their country. It was one thing to release this torrent of young energy, but it was quite another to order or direct it. It is not clear, however, that Mao's intention *was* to order and direct the energies of the enthusiastic young. As he saw it, they were a purging flame that would burn away the bureaucratic shadows whose presence he so abhorred. Once this had been done, the "wisdom of the people" would reassert itself and bureaucracy would never rise again. What FN and NF people have great difficulty in imagining is that any intelligent, able, and "good" person could possibly fail to share their moral vision!

The Red Guards, from their own account, became involved *not* in unified moral actions deriving from Mao's "Little Red Book" but in factional quarrels over what the little book really meant and how its message should be interpreted. Mao's gnomic statements, like any other poetry, are open to many different interpretations, and it appears that some—perhaps much—blood was shed in disputes over them. It does not seem to have struck Mao that the "Little Red Book," like any other politicomoral book, might itself become a source not of unity but of almost infinite dissension.

When the army, and presumably Chou En-lai, stepped in and in a typically Chinese way set about repairing the great damage that the Cultural Revolution had inflicted, they did what could be done to save Mao's face and maintain at least some aspects of his dogma. His objective was excellent. Any rapidly changing society will find the rigidities and heartlessness of bureaucracy every bit as intolerable as the more obvious tyranny of tsar, emperor, or dictator. It is not good enough, however, even with the best of motives, to try to overcome the shortcoming of a bureaucracy by inept and haphazard means. Mao used what he felt were the only means left open to him. His Structural authority was circumscribed, probably rigidly, by the bureaucracy that he may well have intended to eliminate forever. His Sapiential authority had been compromised by the disastrous Great Leap Forward. There is little evidence that he possesses (and a good deal of evidence that he abhors) Stalinesque political manipulative authority. It appears that Mao used his immense Moral and Charismatic authorities without grasping the possibility that if he succeeded in setting things aright with moral fervor for his inspired vision, there might be no way of controlling or directing the flames. Indeed, it sometimes looked as if the Great Leap Forward and Red Guard phases of the Cultural Revolution would resemble Charles Lamb's story of the discovery of roast pork by burning down one's house.

Expansive human beings like Mao are probably as disturbed and distressed by the idea that there are innate and inescapable differences between humans as constricted humans are appalled by the notion that "the Colonel's Lady an' Judy O'Grady are sisters under their skins!" Neither wishes to concede the obvious fact that people can be classified or ordered in terms of differences *and* similarities. Both are "correct" or "incorrect," depending upon how one chooses to look at the problem.

If BBC-TV is correct in its appreciation of the problem, Mao has conferred upon his countrymen the *inverse* of the error made by Western managers who tend to believe that they own their employees body and soul. The Western worker who has been "bought" ceases—both to himself and to his employer—to be a human "partner" in an enterprise; he becomes instead the "cog in the machine," as aptly portrayed in Charlie Chaplin's *Modern Times.* The worker is dehumanized.

Mao perceives the bureaucratic *manager* as the one who is more or less nonhuman. Mao's manager must frequently be reminded of this by having to return to the fields or the workbench to "learn from the workers and peasants." Of the two kinds of errors Mao's seems to be less reprehensible, but he is still making a mistake. This kind of mistake can be avoided only by a better theory of management than Mao's or Adam Smith's. Mao's exemplary and visionary nature told him that something was going very wrong with Chinese management and that this would lead to the subversion of the revolution. His instincts were sound, but one cannot survive on instinct alone, especially under rapidly changing circumstances. Mao's attempt to reconstruct *the present and the future in terms of the past*—the Long March—seems to have failed because it was *bound* to fail.

It would be a grave error on our part not to examine the failure of so great a man with respect and admiration. There is something splendidly human in attempting the impossible.

The Nixon-Kissinger Combination

For some time to come, historians will be arguing about the role of President Nixon's elusive eminence, Henry Kissinger.

Mr. N. is a Sensation-Thinking-type of the Introverted variety. Dr. K. appears to be a Thinking-Intuitive-type who is highly Extraverted (a view confirmed by a colleague who knows him personally). The pair appears to represent a rather well-balanced force; Mr. N.'s Introversion is balanced by Dr. K.'s Extraversion, and the ST's uninspiring qualities can be enlivened by the imaginative and detached TN. Indeed, the White House became a sprightlier place politically once Dr. K. arrived. It is not just that things began happening there, but that interesting, unusual, and original things were happening. A period of lively diplomacy developed, together with the expected criticism both within and without the United States and among both allies and adversaries.

President Nixon's forte clearly lies in the area of his Structural authority. He is a highly manipulative man who is good at getting things done. By his role and his apparent inclination, Dr. Kissinger is a lively Sapiential authority. Have we at last discovered the longed-for but elusive combination of king and philosopher?

There is little doubt that Mr. N. is engaged in the business of kinging, and Dr. K.'s philosophy doctorate entitles him to at least some kind of philosophizing, which he seems to be practicing—he *is* advising the president.

I am *not* convinced—and the flickers of uneasiness that seem to trouble the public psyche over the Nixon-Kissinger alliance suggest that others are not convinced, either—that we are yet in the hands of the optimally wise and humane ruler (albeit a two-headed one, as it were). If one analyzes the pair in typo-methectic terms, there are many clues to the sources of the uneasiness. It is possible to assess the processes or lack of processes that are required for sustaining a workable alliance such as the one between Mr. N. and Dr. K.

The two are well equipped in Thinking and Sensation, less well equipped (but by no means lacking) in Intuition. They are hardly equipped at all in Feeling. The effects this can have on the methectic process can be considerable. According to Paterson's methectics, *information* is collected and studied, *conclusions* are drawn, *decisions* based upon those conclusions are made, and *actions* are taken according to the decisions. In an IST-ETN alliance, such as Mr. N.'s and Dr. K.'s, we are dealing with a system that tends to bypass *conclusions*, which ought to be of three kinds: inspirational, moral, and intellectual. Conclusions of these sorts—converted to decisions and thence to actions—add to the overall process elements of excitement that "feel good" and represent a consensus of sound moral thinking. This sort of thing doesn't often happen, but it is a desirable and—in the gravest of matters, I suspect—an *essential* goal to pursue if commitment to action is to be sustained through time.

The Nixon-Kissinger cycle looks to me as if it would go: information-decision-action, information-decision-action, and so forth, omitting conclusions. It would tend, thus, to be high in feedforward and low in feedback. This would make it produce many deftly executed surprises (as there indeed have been), but the system would be low in *moral solidity*. One would thus never feel that it represented the views of anyone except the king and his philosopher, who are likely therefore—for all their great abilities—to seem manipulative and arrogant when viewed critically. Both (but for quite different reasons) can be expected to enjoy secrecy: the philosopher, because it produces surprises that are likely to astonish; the king, because he knows that this increases the chance of success in manipulation.

And they *are* secretive.

It is debatable whether this sort of system of hasty planning, snap decisions, and precipitate action—lacking sober conclusions, forethought, and moral commitment—will manage to sustain public confidence through bad times and good, as a good philosopher-king should.

Index

About the Authors

Dr. Humphry Osmond is a member of the Royal College of Physicians, London; a holder of the D.P.M. diploma in psychological medicine and a certificate in psychiatry, Royal College of Surgeons and Physicians, of Canada; a founder-member of the Royal College of Psychiatrists, England; a founder-member of the Collegium Internationale Neuro-Psycho-Pharmacoligicum; a fellow member of the World Academy of Arts and Sciences; a founding member of the Academy of Orthomolecular Psychiatry; a consultant on socioarchitectural activities to the governments of the United States and Canada; and director of the Bureau of Research in Neurology and Psychiatry, New Jersey Neuro-Psychiatric Institute, Princeton, New Jersey. He is a coauthor of *The Future of Time* and *The Hallucinogens*. His work includes research in schizophrenia and its many ramifications, appropriate use of psychedelics (he coined the word), and devising means for measuring and exploring the experiential world of human beings.

John A. Osmundsen has for eighteen years been a journalist, communications specialist, lecturer, and writer, principally in science, medicine, and technology, for newspapers (*The San Francisco Chronicle, The New York Times*); magazines (*Life, Look*); radio (WQXR, NBC-Monitor); motion pictures (United Nations, WNBC-TV, industrial); television (Public Broadcasting Laboratory of National Educational Television, WNBC-TV, WCBS-TV, Network for Continuing Medical Education); and public relations (university, foundation, industrial).

Jerome Agel is the author or coauthor and/or producer of: *Herman Kahnsciousness; I Seem to Be a Verb* (with Buckminster Fuller); *The Radical Therapist; Rough Times; The Making of Kubrick's 2001; The Cosmic Connection: An Extraterrestrial Perspective* (with Carl Sagan); *The Medium Is the Massage* and *War and Peace in the Global Village* (with Marshall McLuhan); *The Community Sex Information Guide; Is Today Tomorrow?—A Synergistic Collage of Alternative Futures; A World Without—What Our Presidents Didn't Know; It's About Time.*

74 75 76 77 10 9 8 7 6 5 4 3 2 1